ENGLAND
RUGBY

ENGLAND RUGBY
THE OFFICIAL 2005 YEARBOOK

Published by TRMG Ltd
©2005 TRMG

ISBN 0-9550196-1-3

Smeg UK   information line: Tel 0870 9901902   Fax 0870 9909337   www.smeguk.com
FAB28   50's Style Refrigerators   with Ice Box   Energy Efficiency Class: A

CONTENTS

ENGLAND SEASON REVIEW

A look back at the achievements of our national team and the British & Irish Lions, together with an overview of a season of English domestic rugby

ENGLAND REPRESENTATIVE TEAMS

Relive the exploits of all the other sides that wore the Red Rose with pride in this campaign

RUGBY ROUND-UP

A review of all the other major events in the England Rugby calendar

26

18

JOIN THE ENGLAND RUGBY
SUPPORTERS CLUB NOW!
See page 129 to find out about all
the great benefits you'll receive

10

42

44

WELCOME

By Andy Robinson OBE

Welcome to the England Rugby Yearbook, where I'm sure you will enjoy looking back on what has been a fascinating year for English rugby. England teams at all international levels have been involved in plenty of exciting games and everyone who contributes at every level of the sport has been working extremely hard to develop English rugby for the future. As Head Coach of the national team I have been doing my utmost to make sure our elite side always represents the nation proudly. I must say the players have been magnificent in their desire and hunger to be the very best. They have never wavered in their dedication to the cause and their application simply can't be faulted. As everyone who follows England knows, we've not had our most successful year and had to concede the RBS 6 Nations trophy to Wales. We only managed to finish fourth in the tournament and that was a disappointment, of course. It must be said, however, that our best efforts to deliver consistent success on the pitch have not been helped by disruptions caused by injuries to vital players. Richard Hill and Mike Tindall, key members of my squad, have been unavailable for large parts of the campaign. We lost Jonny Wilkinson for the entire international calendar. Then his replacement as captain, Jason Robinson, was ruled out halfway through our RBS 6 Nations campaign. I was delighted, of course, to see Martin Corry make such an outstanding contribution in replacing Jason as skipper. But nevertheless, a little more stability next season would be most welcome.

That's not to say we haven't had some real positives to take from the 2004-05 season. The emergence of talented new players such as Mark Cueto, Jamie Noon and Olly Barkley has been very satisfying. These guys have proved they have what it takes to compete at the very highest level and have been invaluable.

Away from the international arena, our domestic season was totally enthralling and highly competitive. Enjoy the Yearbook.

Andy Robinson OBE,
England Head Coach

KING COZZA

England skipper Martin Corry should be on top of the world after playing out of his skin in the last year. So why on earth doesn't he ever want another season like this one? Let Howard Johnson explain...

"Of course it's been a tremendous honour. And I look back on it with huge pride. It's been amazing. But you have to put it in perspective. I was made England captain when there were plenty of other top players injured. Jonny Wilkinson. Mike Tindall. Richard Hill. Jason Robinson. I'm under no illusions that if everyone had been fit, then I probably wouldn't have been made captain." Don't be so sure Martin Corry, Zurich Premiership Player of the Season and PRA Players' Player of the Year. If the last season proved anything at all, it's that absolutely anything can happen in sport. And the general rule of thumb is that it usually does.

England Rugby sat down with 'Cozza' to find the Leicester back rower in straight-talking mood. "I don't feel like I'm established," he admitted. "I feel like I've been a fringe player." He was right, too. Under Clive Woodward Corry had found it tough to pierce the established England back row trio of Hill, Back and Dallaglio. But with Back and Dallaglio retiring and Hill sidelined with a long-term

Right:
Always in the thick of the action

Below:
Shocked, stunned and delighted to be named PRA Player of the Season

injury, the likes of Corry, his Leicester team mate Lewis Moody and Wasps man Joe Worsley suddenly found they had a real chance to stake their claims for permanent places in Head Coach Andy Robinson's new regime. Come the end of the 2005 RBS 6 Nations and there was no doubt who'd made the most impact. Martin Corry's season was simply a stormer and whether or not injuries had forced Robinson's hand into appointing him captain for the first time against Italy on March 12, Martin Corry had suddenly become one of the first names pencilled in on any England team sheet. You'd have thought the Leicester man would be pleased as punch with the way things have gone. Well, you would – if you didn't know his fiercely competitive spirit.

"All the good things that happened were personal achievements," he explains.

"Which is very nice and all the rest of it, but they're not what I'm in the game for. Yes, I'm happy with the way I've played this season, but what it's really all about is working hard for the team so that you get your collective rewards. On that score I've failed at both club and international level. Neither England nor the Tigers picked up any trophies for winning competitions, so from that point of view my overriding memory of this season will be that it was one where we stuffed up."

It's a harsh assessment, but as any professional player worth his salt will always tell you, first is first and second is nowhere.

"We've gone through a lot of changes with England as everybody knows," Corry continues. "But if I could be given one single power right now it would be to ban the word 'transition'. I've heard it far too much where England is concerned and now it's getting on my nerves. After the autumn tests and some good performances (a thumping win against Canada, a convincing victory against the Springboks and a narrow defeat to Australia) we all felt confident about what we were doing. But the Six Nations came around and there were more changes because of injuries to key players. But the truth is we didn't cope with that as well as we should. We didn't play well in that tournament. The results we should have been getting weren't there and that was very disappointing. The squad certainly realises that and the will is there to get our heads down and work, to get more cohesiveness into our play for the future. There are still some positives that we can take from our season, though. I think players like Jamie Noon, Ollie Barkley and Mark Cueto were amazing. They've put their hands up and said 'Yes, we can play at this level. We're good enough.' That's going to be a big plus for England next season." Ask him how he's grown during his period as England skipper and Corry will raise one quizzical eyebrow in your direction.

"I don't think I have grown," he claims. "I think I'm pretty much the same old, same old. If there's one thing I learned from playing under Johnno for all those years at Leicester it's that when you're skippering a side it's vital not to try to be something you're not. If it works, it works and if it doesn't, then it doesn't." The media would love to make out that there's a whole lot more to inspirational captaincy than that, though, surely...

"They would, because that gives them more to write about, doesn't it? But besides not asking someone to do something you wouldn't be prepared to do yourself and trying to lead by example, I'm not sure that there is any more to it. I got a lot of people saying 'Oh, didn't he do well' last season. But I'm really not doing too much different to what I was doing before. Maybe my form has been a bit better overall, but you know... I look at a player like Lewis Moody, who I think has been absolutely brilliant for England; he's getting better and better all the time, going from strength to strength. But he didn't seem to be flavour of the month, so he didn't get the press that I really thought he deserved." He's got a point, but surely when your fellow pros vote you their Player of the Season, then you maybe have to accept that you've stepped up a notch or two.

"It was a really big surprise... but a nice

one. Personally I voted for Laurent Chabal from Sale Sharks. I thought he had a massive season. I really wasn't expecting any awards at all and when I turned up for the dinner I was feeling pretty sheepish. I'd just been banned for punching Richard Hill in a league match for Leicester against Saracens and was pretty much feeling like Public Enemy Number One." Ah yes, an unfortunate incident, but one which most who witnessed it thought merited nothing more than a yellow card and a bit of cooling off time in the sin bin.

"Well I don't think I was harshly treated," says Corry, candidly. "There are a lot of criticisms of the disciplinary system in our sport, but once I got sent off they had to do something. At the hearing the committee listened to what I had to say... and then ignored it! Just joking. I accepted my punishment and it was just one of those things. And fair play to Richard's missus. I saw them at a 'do' not so long after the incident and went over to apologise to Richard. She said to me, 'Of all the people who've ever hit Richard, you're the only one I've ever stuck up for.' Which was nice." But missing Leicester's crucial

Heineken Cup semi-final against Stade Toulousain as part of Corry's ban hurt more than any punch ever could.

"It was agony," he admits. "Being up there in the stands, fully fit, and not being able to do a thing about what was happening down on the pitch. Especially when we lost the game. Nightmare. Not that my replacement Henry Tuilagi let the side →

Right:
*Martin put in
some fine
performances
for Leicester,
but ended the
season without
a trophy*

*Far right:
Relaxed as
England
skipper, but
Martin expects
more from
the next
international
campaign*

CORRY

→ down. Far from it. He played phenomenally well. But it just wasn't to be." Martin says missing the Toulouse game is his worst memory of this season. That, and Leicester's 'no show' at the Zurich Premiership Final at Twickenham against Wasps, when the Tigers were never at the races in a 39-14 defeat. "All I kept thinking was that it was Johnno's last game and we were really messing it up for him." But let's not harp on about the negatives.

"My best moment this season was definitely standing in the tunnel in the last few moments before walking out at the head of an England side for the first time. That Italy game will live with me for a long, long time." So tell us. How exactly did it feel?

"It's hard to explain. I think what I was mostly thinking of was all my family who were up in the stands watching. It was nice for them and it was nice for me to see how they reacted, how pleased they were for me." No doubt they felt the same burst of pride when Martin was selected by Sir Clive Woodward for this summer's Lions tour to Australia and then even went on to captain the

Lions. Despite playing in both the first and third Tests in Australia in 2001, this was the first time that Corry had been selected for the original squad. He was called up four years ago as cover for the injured Simon Taylor.

"Our job next season is to make sure that we put everything we've

learnt in the last season to good use and for England to come back stronger and to start winning tournaments again." Regardless of whether you're England skipper or not? Cozza doesn't hesitate. "Well, you don't even need me to answer that one, surely..." he says.

TO FIND YOUR NEAREST STOCKISTS
CALL 01753 497100

Face up to it!

BET EURO

SEASON 2

And what a season it was! Relive everything that mattered in the English game – internationals, domestic competition, England's Lions – in our massive 36 page review section

ENGLAND V CANADA

Saturday November 13, 2004

Twickenham

England 70 Canada 0

WORDS: MATTHEW JACKS

Andy Robinson went into his first game as England Head Coach determined that opponents Canada would witness first hand a new brand of English rugby. The national team had shed much of its old foliage by the time Robinson had moved into the hot seat to replace Sir Clive Woodward, and the retirement of eight key men – not to mention long term injuries to elite players such as

Jonny Wilkinson, Phil Vickery and Richard Hill – had left England entering a clear transitional phase.

Nevertheless, Robinson was determined that such major upheavals wouldn't stop him from sending out a side – led for the first time by Sale Sharks man Jason Robinson – that was brimming with attacking intent. And Robinson the player was in no mood to show mercy, notching a hat trick of

tries in less than an hour to earn himself the 'Man of the Match' accolade.

In fact, it was a red letter day all round for Sale's England boys. Mark Cueto scored a brace of tries on his debut and fly half Charlie Hodgson also helped himself to one to compensate for five missed conversions from 12 attempts. The game also provided a solid start for Robinson's 'New' England.

ENGLAND V SOUTH AFRICA

Saturday November 20, 2004
Twickenham
England 32 South Africa 16

WORDS: MATTHEW JACKS

New Springboks coach Jake White had rid his side of the rough-house tactics which had marred their last visit to Twickenham back in 2002 and all the pre-match talk centred on Schalk Burger, South Africa's blonde blindside dynamo and soon-to-be IRB Player of the Year.

It quickly emerged, though, that a less-heralded figure in the home team's back row was in no mood to respect reputations. Martin Corry was desperate to enhance his own international standing after a lifetime spent behind Lawrence Dallaglio, Neil Back and Richard Hill axis. And the Leicester Tigers man put in a colossal performance which quickly shattered Burger's brightly burning star and the Boks' aura of frightening forward physicality.

Playing on the front foot thanks to Corry's impressive ball carrying, Charlie Hodgson also enjoyed one of his best games ever in an England shirt. He wriggled over for a fine solo effort under the sticks and kicked two conversions, five penalties and a drop goal. His fellow stand off Jonny Wilkinson, sitting watching in the stands because of injury, would certainly have been impressed by the Sale Sharks' man's performance. Another Shark, Mark Cueto, was also setting Twickenham alight for the second successive weekend. He expertly gathered Henry Paul's cross field kick for England's other score and Bryan Habana's late consolation for a jaded South Africa did nothing to dampen English elation at a fine win.

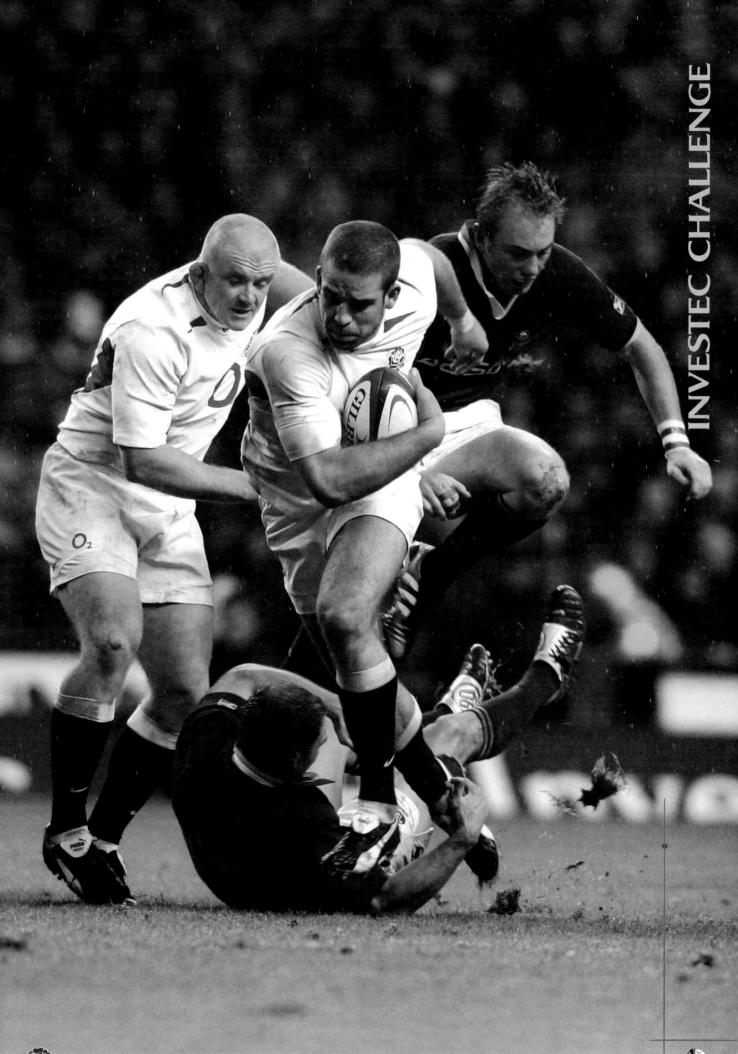

ENGLAND V AUSTRALIA

Saturday November 27, 2004

Twickenham

England 19 Australia 21

Described by his peers as possessing the skills of Stephen Larkham and the speed of Tim Horan at his best, Wallabies centre Matt Giteau was always going to be seen as a rugby cocktail determined to shake up England in the last of their three Investec Challenge autumn internationals. And so it proved as the home nation, despite starting the match at an admirably high tempo, were stung by two first-half tries brilliantly created by the Wallabies' number 12.

A rapid turn of pace from Giteau left Joe Worsley grasping at thin air as hooker Jeremy Paul was put in for the first score, before a pin-point Giteau pass then found Chris Latham on the charge to run in Australia's second. The red rose boys were clearly rocked and Andy Robinson acted promptly by replacing Henry Paul with Will Greenwood with less than half an hour of the game gone.

A penalty slotted shortly after the interval took Australia 15-0 up and there really appeared to be no way back for England. But the home pack took a deep breath and hauled the team back into the contest, creating tries for both Lewis Moody and Josh Lewsey after energy-sapping rolling mauls had taken their toll on the Australian defence.

It was an immense effort and England's comeback looked complete when Cueto finished off a peach of a backs move to take Robinson's men into an incredible 18-15 lead.

But some earlier missed kicks and poor ball retention under pressure in the latter stages were to cost England dear as the Wallabies slotted two late penalties and grabbed victory from underneath English noses. Despite plenty of positives in the game, fortress Twickenham had been breached at the death.

WORDS: MATTHEW JACKS

FREE LIONS TOUR TEE SHIRT*
worth £14.99

FREE

The Lions Replica Jersey L/S
red/white
size: s & l - 3xl
£54.99

The Lions Replica Jersey S/S
red/white
size: s - 3xl
£49.99

FREE LIONS BACKPACK*
worth £14.99

FREE

The Lions Youth Replica Jersey S/S
size: sb - xlb
£39.99

The Lions Infant Replica Jersey L/S
size: 20/22, 22/24, 24/26
£27.99

FREE LIONS BACKPACK*
worth £14.99

FREE

The Lions Training Jerseys 1, 2 & 3 Kids
white, green & navy
size: sb - xlb
£34.99

FREE LIONS SCARF*
worth £11.99

FREE

The Lions Training Jersey 1
white
size: s - 3xl
£44.99

FREE LIONS SCARF*
worth £11.99

FREE

The Lions Training Jersey 2
green
size: s - 3xl
£44.99

FREE LIONS SCARF*
worth £11.99

FREE

The Lions Training Jersey 3
navy
size: s - 3xl
£44.99

The Lions Presentation Track Suit
red/navy
size: m - 2xl
£69.99

The Lions Replica Shorts
white
size: 30" - 44"
£17.99

The Lions Training Shorts
navy/green
size: 30" 32" 36" 38" 40" 42"
£17.99

Limited Edition
Exclusive to rugbystore.co.uk

The Lions Ltd. Edition Training Shorts
navy/red
size: 30" - 44"
£17.99

Gilbert Xact Lions Matchball
size: 5
£64.99

Gilbert Lions Tour Dates Ball
size: 5
£12.99

The Lions Windbreaker
navy/red
size: s - 2xl
£39.99

The Lions Replica Socks
navy/green
size: 6-8, 81
£12.99
size: 4-6
£10.99

Gilbert Lions Replica Ball
size: 5
£19.99

Gilbert Lions Super Midi Ball
size: midi
£9.99

The Lions Woven Shorts
navy/white
size: 30" - 44"
£17.99

*****While stocks last**

rugbystore.co.uk
25 Market Street
Galashiels, TD1 3AF

FREEPHONE HOTLINES OPEN:
Monday - Friday 8am - 5:30pm,
Saturday 9am - 5pm, Sunday midday - 4pm
P&P: £4.11 (UK) per order for any number of items

rugbystore.co.uk

The Lions No. 13 Jersey
navy/green
size: s - 2xl
£44.99

The Lions No. 10 Jersey
white/red
size: s - 2xl
£44.99

The Lions Polo Shirt
red
size: s - 3xl
£24.99

The Lions Polo Shirt
white
size: s - 3xl
£24.99

The Lions Polo Shirt
navy
size: s - 3xl
£24.99

The Lions Performance Tee
navy/red
size: s - 3xl
£17.99

The Lions Fleece Top
red/navy
size: s - 2xl
£37.99

The Lions 'Last Man Standing' Tee
red
size: s - 2xl
£13.99

The Lions Hooded Top
navy/red
size: xl & 2xl
£34.99

The Lions 'Tour Dates' Power Trip Tee
red or navy
size: s - 2xl
£14.99

BACK IN STOCK
Limited Availability

The Lions Baby Kit
red/white
6/9, 12 & 18 month
£19.99

The Lions Classic Tee
red/navy
size: s, xl & 2xl
£17.99

1. **Beenie Hat**
2. **Dive Cap**
3. **Basic 3S**
£9.99

The Lions Backpack
navy/red
£14.99

The Lions Teambag
navy/red
£19.99

Lions Tie
poly: **£14.99**
Lions Tie - Stripe
poly: **£14.99**
silk: **£27.99**

1. **Mini Ball**
£5.99
2. **Stress Ball**
3. **Key Ring**
£2.50

Adidas The Lions Supporters Scarf
£11.99
The Lions Lambswool scarf
£24.99

Lions Towel
£14.99
Lions Mug
£5.99

Lions Beenie Bear
£5.99
Lions Water Bottle
£3.99
Lions Pin Badge
£2.99

RBS 6 NATIONS 2005

Wales won the Grand Slam, England finished fourth. It certainly wasn't our most successful campaign, but Andy Robinson's rebuilding process gathered pace...

WORDS: MATTHEW JACKS

England won't look back on their 2005 RBS 6 Nations as anything like a vintage campaign. But there were still enough positives to encourage Head Coach Andy Robinson as he continued the building process towards the ultimate goal of World Cup glory in 2007.

Young Matthew Stevens, 22, made his first start in an England jersey against Ireland at Lansdowne Road and caught the eye with a top class scrummaging display.

Martin Corry continued to deliver high quality performances at the back of the pack and proved he'd picked up a few leadership tips from long-time Leicester colleague Martin Johnson along the way. Mark Cueto finished as the tournament's top try scorer with five touchdowns. And on the other flank Josh Lewsey continued to be top class in both attack and defence.

With Stevens, scrum half Harry Ellis and centre Jamie Noon all demonstrating their true international calibre, the long-term prospects properly blooded during this tournament may well compensate in the future for a lack of tangible success on the field in 2005. And even then England did come within four minutes of beating Wales, the eventual Grand Slam champions in the opening game. Had that tournament-defining result gone the other way, who's to say what would have happened?

WALES V ENGLAND

A Whisker Away From Glory

Saturday February 5, 2005

Millennium Stadium, Cardiff

Wales 11 England 9

I t was always going to be a close shave – and that's without taking Gavin Henson's penchant for personal grooming into account. England travelled to Cardiff, where they hadn't lost for 12 years, on the back of an encouraging autumn. But the Six Nations saw England deprived of a whole host of stars.

Lewis Moody's withdrawal due to hamstring trouble just 24 hours before kick off was typical of England's bad luck. Andy Robinson selected just five members of the 2003 World Cup winning team, though one of those players was scrum half Matt Dawson, returning to the fold after missing the autumn internationals.

Wales sensed a chance to draw first blood in the tournament, especially after the shoots of recovery first evident in Australia had been further developed under new coach Mike Ruddock. Both South Africa and New Zealand had been run close in the autumn and the overriding feeling in the Principality was that a major scalp was there for the taking.

The home side were rewarded for their overall superiority when Shane Williams crossed for what proved to be the only try of the match on 11 minutes. The Red Dragon was roaring and the pressure cooker atmosphere was turned up another couple of notches. Could England front up and match the home side for spirit and endeavour? Well, yes they could. It was even stevens and nip and tuck all through the match, with neither side able to gain that crucial advantage.

Three Charlie Hodgson penalties threatened to spoil Wales' day. Gavin Henson, however, was desperate to rid his side of their 'nearly men' tag and coolly slotted a long-range penalty in the 74th minute to break England's resolve and get the Red Dragons' tournament off to a flyer.

ENGLAND V FRANCE

Defeat Snatched From The Jaws Of Victory

Sunday February 13, 2005

Twickenham

England 17 France 18

Sir Clive Woodward often talked about the 'brutal reality' of international sport, how the margins between glorious victory and miserable defeat can be measured in inches. On this day England found out exactly what he meant by that. Charlie Hodgson missed three attempts at goal before handing over the responsibility to Bath's Olly Barkley, who then conspired to miss three penalties of his own. France were well and truly let off the hook and to add insult to injury, they then went on to steal an improbable victory.

In the proverbial games of two halves England dominated the first 40 minutes and scored two well-worked tries to build a comfortable 17-6 lead. Barkley, who had come into the side, was on hand to benefit from centre partner Jamie Noon's surging run and score the first try, before winger Josh Lewsey used his pace to outstrip French defensive cover for the second. Hodgson converted both scores and added a penalty, but the 11-point lead was in truth a poor reflection of the home side's ascendancy.

France had forgotten to show up in the first half, but turned the game on its head in the second period with a far more focused display. England, on the other hand, lost their shape and discipline. A succession of penalties awarded against them proved well within the range of scrum half Dimitri Yachvili, who proved to be in deadly form with the boot, landing four penalties to add to the two he'd slotted in the first period. Yachvili's efforts completed a remarkable turnaround for Les Bleus and a miserable afternoon for England. A game which had started so brightly had ended in sheer frustration. And no England fan could quite believe it.

IRELAND V ENGLAND

So Close... And Yet So Far

Sunday February 27, 2005
Lansdowne Road, Dublin
Ireland 19 England 13

Refereeing standards were a hot topic in the week leading up to England's match in Ireland. Northampton coach Budge Pountney was hit in the pocket and banned from match day coaching for six weeks for calling a Zurich Premiership referee "a disgrace". But little did anyone know just how hot a topic it would become in the aftermath of England's 19-13 defeat at Lansdowne Road.

Mark Cueto had a first half effort harshly disallowed for being in front of Charlie Hodgson after he'd gathered his Sale team mate's cross-field kick and flopped over the line. And worse was to follow when Kaplan did not consult video official Huw Watkins when Josh Lewsey looked to have touched down under a pile of bodies at a critical point in the second period. England showed great determination in putting these incidents behind them and were highly competitive for the whole of an enthralling game. Andy Robinson's men battled valiantly and matched Ireland's obvious passion for the fight every step of the way, but despite their best endeavours the rub of the green simply wouldn't go their way.

A piece of try-scoring magic from Brian O'Driscoll and 15 points from the boot of Ronan O'Gara condemned England to their worst start to a championship campaign since 1987. Andy Robinson was understandably fuming after the match. The England Head Coach was rightly quick to praise the sterling efforts of his side in every department, but on this particular occasion it simply wasn't to be. Another game that England could so easily have won had somehow slipped through their fingers. It was hard for all red rose supporters to take.

ENGLAND V ITALY

That Winning Feeling Again

Saturday March 12, 2005
Twickenham
England 39 Italy 7

While Josh Lewsey had warned it would take England a good 18 months to become the best in the world again, everyone expected the side to get back to winning ways against Italy. But Andy Robinson was once again forced into changes as a torn thumb ligament ruled Jason Robinson out for the rest of the tournament. England hopeful Ben Cohen also saw his chances of re-establishing himself in the side cut short because of a broken jaw sustained in the Tsunami aid match at Twickenham a week earlier.

Martin Corry was a popular choice as Robinson's replacement to lead England out and his first match in charge ended with a satisfactory win. Italy were no match for England. Mark Cueto's rapidly growing reputation as a deadly finisher gained further momentum with a hat-trick of tries, taking his tally to an impressive seven scores in seven matches since his debut in November 2004.

Full back Iain Balshaw also announced his arrival back on the international scene with a well-taken try to cap a fine all-round game, and there were further scores for hooker Steve Thompson and flanker Andy Hazell as England happily rediscovered that lovely winning feeling. A good day all round.

ENGLAND V SCOTLAND

Moving On Up

Saturday March 19, 2005

Twickenham

England 43 Scotland 22

Would he or wouldn't he? A potential Jonny Wilkinson comeback had never been far away from everyone's thoughts throughout the RBS 6 Nations. Speculation as to his likely return date, first for club and then for country, dominated the newspapers' back pages alongside the matches.

Wilkinson finally proved his fitness to Newcastle and took to the field for the Falcons in their league match against NEC Harlequins at the Stoop. If he came through that challenge unscathed, then the smart money was on Wilkinson making a swift return to south west London to warm the bench against Scotland a week later. But Wilkinson lasted just 34 minutes of his comeback match after receiving a blow to the same left knee that had kept him sidelined for the previous eight weeks. There would be no Jonny for England during this year's RBS 6 Nations. Still, it was one of Newcastle's own who stole the show at Twickenham.

With Wales already bagging the Grand Slam just over an hour earlier, England's finale against Scotland threatened to be an anti-climax. But centre Jamie Noon's stunning hat-trick and tries for Mark Cueto, Joe Worsley, Josh Lewsey and Harry Ellis, combined with a spirited display from Scotland, made for an entertaining end to England's Six Nations campaign as the home side showed its attacking teeth. Andy Robinson would have looked back on England's final display as indicative of his team's tournament; plenty of good things, but also plenty to work on in the ongoing evolution of English international rugby.

FINAL STANDINGS									
TEAM	**PLD**	**W**	**D**	**L**	**PF**	**PA**	**DIFF**	**BP**	**PTS**
WALES	5	5	0	0	151	77	74	0	10
FRANCE	5	4	0	1	134	82	52	0	8
IRELAND	5	3	0	2	126	101	25	0	6
ENGLAND	5	2	0	3	121	77	44	0	4
SCOTLAND	5	1	0	4	84	155	-71	0	2
ITALY	5	0	0	5	55	179	-124	0	0

RESULTS					
DATE	**VENUE**	**HOME**	**H**	**A**	**AWAY**
5-Feb-05	Stade de France	FRANCE	16	9	SCOTLAND
5-Feb-05	Cardiff Millennium	WALES	11	9	ENGLAND
6-Feb-05	Rome	ITALY	17	28	IRELAND
12-Feb-05	Rome	ITALY	8	38	WALES
12-Feb-05	Murrayfield	SCOTLAND	13	40	IRELAND
13-Feb-05	Twickenham	ENGLAND	17	18	FRANCE
26-Feb-05	Murrayfield	SCOTLAND	18	10	ITALY
26-Feb-05	Stade de France	FRANCE	18	24	WALES
27-Feb-05	Lansdowne Road	IRELAND	19	13	ENGLAND
12-Mar-05	Lansdowne Road	IRELAND	19	26	FRANCE
12-Mar-05	Twickenham	ENGLAND	39	7	ITALY
13-Mar-05	Murrayfield	SCOTLAND	22	46	WALES
19-Mar-05	Rome	ITALY	13	56	FRANCE
19-Mar-05	Cardiff Millennium	WALES	32	20	IRELAND
19-Mar-05	Twickenham	ENGLAND	43	22	SCOTLAND

SIX NATIONS. ONE PASSION.

rbs6nations.com

Make it happen

The Royal Bank of Scotland Group

ENGLAND V BARBARIANS

13 Try Spectacular: Saturday 28 May 2005, Twickenham,

England 39 Barbarians 52

WORDS: JUSTIN O'REGAN

Clockwise from top: James Forrester touches down; Wendell Sailor celebrates one of his brace of tries; The Baa Baas bite at England's ankles; Jamie Noon takes on Thomas Castaignede

The annual clash against the Barbarians has become a crucial proving ground for aspiring England players in recent years and the 2005 TIBCO Challenge was no exception as the Twickenham faithful were treated to a free-flowing 13-try spectacular.

That the final score read 52-39 in the Barbarians' favour was certainly no disgrace for the men in white. Not only were England deprived of their Lions contingent, but their opponents boasted an extraordinary 753 international caps between them and included such luminaries as Wallaby winger Wendell Sailor, All Black and Northampton maestro Bruce Reihana and Springbok flyer Brent Russell amongst their ranks.

This dynamic Baa Baas trio dominated proceedings at the Home of England rugby. They grabbed two tries apiece as the Barbarians made their experience count. Sailor in particular caught the eye with several powerful surges down the touchline that amply demonstrated his lethal attacking credentials.

As you'd expect from a team led by the inspirational figure of Worcester Warriors flanker Pat Sanderson, England refused to be intimidated by

the illustrious invitational side facing them and gave as good as they got for long stretches of what was a highly entertaining match.

With a solid effort from the front five, England were able to create plenty of scoring opportunities of their own, Wasps winger Paul Sackey finding his way over the tryline on two occasions and Ayoola Erinle, James Forrester and Sanderson himself also getting their names on the scoresheet.

While obviously disappointed in defeat, England coach Joe Lydon found plenty of positives in the

performance of his young side. "The experience is vital," he said. "But if you give world class players time, space and opportunities, then they will take them. That's a lesson our players will have to learn."

Gartmore. Barbarians. Two teams. One spirit.

Gartmore are proud to sponsor the Barbarians.
Like us, the Barbarians have a hand-picked team
from the best players in their field.

To find out what Gartmore can do for you,
call 0800 289 336 or visit www.gartmore.co.uk

Gartmore. For investment solutions.

A relentless search for opportunity

WINNERS!

With star performers on Lions duty, Canada's Churchill Cup gave potential England regulars the chance to show their skills. It was a chance they took superbly...

If he'd been around to witness it, the man who gave his name to the annual Churchill Cup would undoubtedly have approved of England's enterprise and daring spirit throughout the 2005 tournament held in Edmonton, Canada in June.

The men in white were fully prepared to see their way to victory as they disposed of Canada, 29-5, and then Argentina, 45-16, to reclaim the trophy they first won in 2003.

Despite being shorn of many of their established Six Nations stars for this tournament England, coached by Joe Lydon, came through their North American adventure with flying colours, the team owing much of their success to a flowing gameplan which put the emphasis firmly on positive, attacking rugby, as their overall tally of 10 tries in two games aptly demonstrates.

And while all but one of those tries were scored by members of England's backline contingent – inspirational skipper Pat Sanderson the only forward to get himself on the scoresheet – the contribution of the men up front to the team's success should not be underestimated. The England pack provided the rock solid platform needed to allow their more fleet-footed comrades to do some serious damage to opponents out wide.

England began their campaign with an awkward opener against a streetwise and physical Canadian side, Sanderson's men sticking to their task well as they waged a war of attrition for long stretches of the match. The continued application of pressure eventually began to open up some cracks in the Canucks' defence and winger Paul Sackey raced away for the first try of the game.

Scoring a further four tries in a somewhat bad-tempered affair, England finished up as 29-5 victors to set up a title decider with Argentina, who had earlier booked a place in the final with a narrow 34-30 victory over the USA Eagles.

Seemingly oblivious to Argentina's reputation as the masters of the set piece, England immediately set about dismantling their opponents' forward efforts, starting the final in dominant mood, the front row trio in particular making life very uncomfortable for the Pumas.

With Tom Palmer and Louis Deacon ruling the air in the lineouts, England's sparkling backline was soon enjoying plenty of possession, allowing the likes of Mathew Tait, James Simpson-Daniel and Tom Voyce the chance to demonstrate their fine attacking credentials.

It was Voyce who was the pick of the crop, his

excellent angled support lines and elusive running skills striking deep into the heart of Argentina territory. The London Wasps man finished the match with two tries to his credit.

Voyce's virtuoso performance was supplemented by further tries from Simpson-Daniel, Sackey and Andy Gomarsall as England's 15-man game created acres of prime attacking space.

With the steady goalkicking of Leicester Tigers fly half Andy Goode underpinning the win, it all adds up to a healthy picture for English rugby when the Churchill Cup winners are thrown back into the mix with the Lions contingent for the upcoming November internationals.

"It's all about winning, but the long-term picture is we need to assess these players and how they come together as a unit," said a delighted Lydon. "We also need to see if they fit into our plans for 2007.

"You only need to look back to see how successful these development squads have been. The amount of players who travelled to North America in 2001 and then went on to play in the World Cup or on the current Lions tour shows what a springboard it is.

"Since the start of the Churchill Cup many of the players who've competed have gone on to become England regulars. Players realise this is an opportunity to set themselves up."

Certainly a whole host of players, most particularly Tom Voyce, Louis Deacon, Perry Freshwater and James Simpson-Daniel, have all strengthened their test claims for the coming season and beyond.

Above left:
Fly half Andy Goode shows some fierce determination against Argentina

Below left:
Pat Sanderson touches down against Canada

ZURICH PREMIERSHIP

DOMESTIC ACTION

With no World Cup to disrupt proceedings, this season's Zurich Premiership should have been about restoring order to rugby's top table. To a certain extent that's what happened. Leicester Tigers, inspired by Head Coach John Wells and the retiring Martin Johnson and Neil Back, began in exactly the same sparkling form they'd shown in the latter part of the previous season. They stormed to the top of the table early on and proved themselves impossible to dislodge come the end of the season. Wasps did their very best to mount a real challenge – and even made it to the top of the pile at certain points – but the Tigers were simply too strong over the course of the campaign.

The most exciting story of the season, though, was taking place at the other end of the table. This time around there was no Rotherham, a team stranded at the bottom of the table from the start and unlikely ever to claw its way out of trouble. Instead, season 2004-05 saw five sides in constant danger of relegation and a scrap which was so tight that even on the very last day nothing definite had been decided.

Why? Well this time we had Worcester taking their bow in the Premiership after earning promotion the previous season. Backed by good finances, with quality coaches (John Brain and Andy Keast) and a solid squad, from the off the Warriors showed a desire to break the mould

FINAL ZURICH PREMIERSHIP TABLE

Position	Team	PLD	PD	PTS
1	Leicester	22	342	78
2	Wasps	22	119	73
3	Sale	22	71	60
4	Bath	22	41	58
5	Saracens	22	-44	57
6	Gloucester	22	-80	47
7	Newcastle	22	-121	47
8	Leeds	22	-51	43
9	Worcester	22	-128	42
10	London Irish	22	-43	40
11	Northampton	22	-63	40
12	Harlequins	22	-43	38

and really compete. When they recorded a 27-24 win against the mighty Wasps it soon became apparent that no one should take the new boys lightly.

That London Irish and Leeds Tykes were in amongst the stragglers didn't come as a huge surprise, perhaps. But the sight of Northampton Saints battling against the drop was a real shock. After enjoying the steady leadership of Wayne Smith, the Saints went into freefall under Alan Solomons and it wasn't until his South African revolution was called to a halt and Budge Pountney and Paul Grayson stepped into the coaching breach that the side finally pulled themselves together. Still, there was plenty of nail

biting from Saints fans during their final game against Worcester, when the unthinkable was still possible.

As tough as Northampton's season was, they always had Harlequins for company. The London club has flirted with disaster often enough, but to fall so spectacularly just one season after taking sixth place was still incredible. Quins had let solid players such as Paul Burke, Pat Sanderson and Chris Bell depart the club (the latter two even moved to relegation rivals) and the lack of depth in the squad was apparent. And while they did pick up points when other sides had players on international duty, Quins didn't do the business when it really mattered. Three consecutive defeats to

struggling Northampton Saints, London Irish and Leeds Tykes proved the point well enough. One final defeat to Sale Sharks sealed their fate and Harlequins – to the surprise of many – will be performing in National One next season.

It really was gripping stuff all round, and there was even more excitement elsewhere in the table. Sale Sharks managed to nick the third play-off spot behind Leicester and Wasps at the expense of Bath, while a rejuvenated Saracens led a mid-table that also included an unusually quiet Gloucester side and a bright Newcastle Falcons outfit who started the season impressively, but faded away towards the end.

Above left:
Bath just missed out on a play off spot, while Leeds Tykes battled their way out of relegation trouble

Left:
This season saw the retirement of Leicester legends Neil Back and Martin Johnson

ZURICH PREMIERSHIP FINAL

Saturday May 14, 2005
Twickenham
Leicester Tigers 14 London Wasps 39

It would have been a brave man indeed who would have bet against Leicester Tigers in the Zurich Premiership Final. Having led the league pretty much from the word go, it was only logical that the Tigers would take the trophy at Twickenham, wasn't it? And with Martin Johnson, Neil Back and Head Coach John Wells all departing (Johnson to retirement, Back to a coaching position at the club and Wells to the RFU) and the Tigers having just whipped opponents Wasps 45-10 in the league, thereby condemning their rivals to second place, few expected the trophy holders

from London to have much of a say in the day's proceedings. How wrong they were.

After failing to truly ignite since their own Heineken Cup Final victory last season, Wasps decided to ruin the party for the Welford Road outfit, finding some stunning form at just the right time. Full back Mark van Gisbergen, who will soon qualify to play for England, put in an inspiring performance and racked up 26 points. Lawrence Dallaglio played like a man possessed. And despite experiencing the hand of Back, Joe Worsley was outstanding as the Londoners – who'd seen off Sale Sharks 43-22 in the semi-final – proved they know a thing or two about play offs and ran out deserved 39-14 winners. It has to be said that the Tigers did everything in their power to hand the trophy to Wasps. The league's most consistent team simply went missing on the big day and never looked like winning. Nevertheless, it was a great way for Wasps coach Warren Gatland to sign off before returning to his native New Zealand.

In the wild card play offs that preceded the main event, Saracens demonstrated their improvement under Steve Diamond by seeing off a spirited challenge from Gloucester by a scoreline of 24-16. The result guaranteed Saracens a place among Europe's elite next season, but also ended Gloucester coach Nigel Melville's reign at Kingsholm.

Above:
Dallaglio and
Johnson:
Legends of
the game

WORDS: PHILIP KIRK

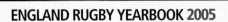

POWERGEN CUP FINAL

Saturday April 16, 2005
Twickenham
Leeds Tykes 20 Bath Rugby 12

This season's Powergen Cup competition proved to be one that won't be forgotten in a long while. It gave us controversy from the very start. Who, for example, would have

thought that London Wasps' 43-33 win over Bristol would be chalked off after the Premiership team fielded an illegal player? Wasps were also cut from the tournament; Bristol heaved a sigh of relief and went through to the next round. There was no fairytale ending for them, though. Local rivals Gloucester saw to that. But there was a very happy ending for one underdog in the Powergen.

Leeds Tykes belied their lowly league position throughout the tournament and duly marched all the way to the final, defeating relegation rivals London Irish and Northampton Saints along the way. On the other side of the draw, meanwhile, cup kings Bath again made it to Twickenham, having beaten both Harlequins and Sale Sharks to get there, the latter by a single point margin. They then defeated old enemy Gloucester in the semi-final in an enthralling encounter.

Roared on by its marching army of cider drinkers, Bath – 10 times finalists, 10 times winners – were the hottest of hot favourites for this year's final. And with Leeds sitting at the very bottom of the Zurich Premiership table at the time, it wasn't hard to see why. But it's with good reason that 'The Magic Of The Cup' has become a clichéd phrase. This was very much the day of the underdog. Bath dominated territory, but didn't seem able to use it to their advantage. Leeds had no such hesitancy in making Bath pay.

A try from new England boy Chris Bell and another breakaway score from former Springbok Andre Snyman, coupled with the coolest of kicking from Scottish fly half Gordon Ross, saw the northerners take the cup by a remarkable 20-12 scoreline.

The Yorkshire club's win formed the backbone of an inspired end to the season for Phil Davies' men, as wins over Gloucester, Leicester, Harlequins and Bath again in the league saw the Tykes stave off relegation too. No one can say they didn't deserve it.

WORDS: PHILIP KIRK

SUBSCRIPTION OFFER

★ Receive 4 issues per year, at a special price of £12.95

★ Free direct delivery to your door, before it hits the newstands

- **Call: 01858 43 88 17**
- **Fax: 01858 46 17 39**
- **Fill in the form below**
- **www.subscription.co.uk/englandrugby/3013**

Subscription Order Form

Please fill in the form and send to: England Rugby, TRMG Subscriptions, FREEPOST, NATE299, Market Harborough, LE16 9ZY.

Title _____ Initial _____ Surname _____

Address _____

_____

_____ Postcode _____

Telephone number _____

e-mail _____

☐ Yes, I would like to subscribe to **England Rugby** for 4 issues at the price of £12.95

I enclose a cheque for £_____ made payable to TRMG Ltd.

Please charge my debit/credit card £ _____

Please (✔) tick applicable: Master Card ☐   Visa ☐   Switch ☐   Delta ☐

Card No. ☐☐☐☐ ☐☐☐☐ ☐☐☐☐ ☐☐☐☐

Valid from ☐☐/☐☐   Expiry date ☐☐/☐☐   Issue No. ☐

Signature _____ Date _____

Subscriptions hotline, 01858 438817 (Monday–Friday, 8.00am–9.30pm – Sat 8.00am–4.00pm), or fax to 01858 461739 www.subscription.co.uk/englandrugby
Quoting Reference: 3013

Please tick the box if you DO NOT wish you details to be used by TRMG Ltd to let you know about our other products and services ☐

Please tick the box if you DO NOT wish to receive information about products and services from other carefully selected companies ☐

☐ **Yes, I would like to subscribe to England Rugby for £12.95 annually and pay by Direct Debit**

Instruction to your bank/building society to pay by Direct Debits.
Please fill in the form and send to:
TRMG Ltd, Tower House, Sovereign Park,
Market Harborough, Leicestershire LE16 9EF

DIRECT Debit

To the manager (Bank name) _____

Address _____

_____

_____ Postcode_____

Name of Account holder(s)

Bank/building society account number: Bank sort code

☐☐☐☐☐☐☐☐   ☐☐ ☐☐ ☐☐

Signature

Date

Reference: 405988

Instruction to your Bank or Building Society. Please pay TRMG Ltd Direct Debits from the account detailed in this instruction subject to the safeguards assured by Direct Debit Guarantee. I understand that this instruction may remain with TRMG Ltd, and, if so, details may be passed electronically to my bank/building society.

Banks and Building Societies may not accept Direct Debit instructions from certains types of account.

PLAYING FOR PRIDE

The British & Irish Lions went to New Zealand full of hope, but they came up against an awesome New Zealand...

I t started with an enjoyable waltz in the opening 15 minutes against Bay Of Plenty but by the end of the tour The British & Irish Lions had found that rugby life is never tougher than in New Zealand. Early tries from sweeping crossfield moves in that tour opener for England stars Josh Lewsey and Mark Cueto promised so much ahead of the stiffer tasks that lay in wait. But the Lions came up against an All Blacks side playing what can only be described as inspirational rugby.

Significant injuries obviously played a part in the Lions' downfall and no one could have predicted the departure of Lawrence Dallaglio just 19 minutes into the tour. Indeed, if the effects of the tackle on skipper Brian O'Driscoll in the first minute of the first test were like a knife through the heart of the massed ranks of Lions supporters, the loss of Dallaglio with a fracture dislocation of his right ankle can't be understated. While the London Wasps man's eventual replacement, Harrogate-raised Ireland international Simon Easterby, went on to turn in a 'Man of the Match' display in the second test, the All Blacks' star-studded back line would surely not have had anything like the quick ball they commanded in

putting the Lions to the sword in all three tests.

Despite a tour de force from Charlie Hodgson in the 36-14 win over Taranaki there continued to be more questions than answers asked of Clive Woodward's men ahead of the first serious challenge, which was to come from the New Zealand Maori. With the Lions struggling to find a coherent style Woodward had plenty of weighty issues on his mind – and that's disregarding his selection of the heaviest front row in Lions history in the 54 stone 10lbs combined forms of the all-English Andrew Sheridan, Steve Thompson and Julian White. Sadly, the Lions came up well short of expectations. "We've got no complaints, the better side won. I think the scoreline flattered us," was Woodward's honest assessment of his side's 19-13 defeat. It was the earliest Lions tour loss since the 1983 whitewash and the first by the Maori after seven previous attempts.

Hard-fought wins against Wellington and Otago got the Lions back on track before the focus switched inevitably to Jonny Wilkinson as Woodward announced his first test XV. Wilkinson's selection at inside centre for the first time in an international since 1999 ahead of Gavin Henson – who responded with two tries against Southland – led to much heated debate. But Wilkinson's centre partner

in the opening test, skipper Brian O'Driscoll, was in no doubt about the merits in selecting Wilkinson at 12. "World class is world class and that's what Jonny is," he said. "He fills everyone around him with confidence and is just a joy to play with."

Unfortunately for the Lions, the

WORDS: MATTHEW JACKS

BRITISH & IRISH LIONS – NEW ZEALAND 2005

Saturday 4 June
Bay Of Plenty 20-34 Lions

Wednesday 8 June
Taranaki 14-36 Lions

Saturday 11 June
NZ Maori 19-13 Lions

Wednesday 15 June
Wellington 6-23 Lions

Saturday 18 June
Otago 19-30 Lions

Tuesday 21 June
Southland 16-26 Lions

Saturday 25 June
New Zealand 21-3 Lions

Tuesday 28 June
Manawatu 6-109 Lions

Saturday 2 July
New Zealand 48-18 Lions

Tuesday 5 July
Auckland 13-17 Lions

Saturday 9 July
New Zealand 38-19 Lions

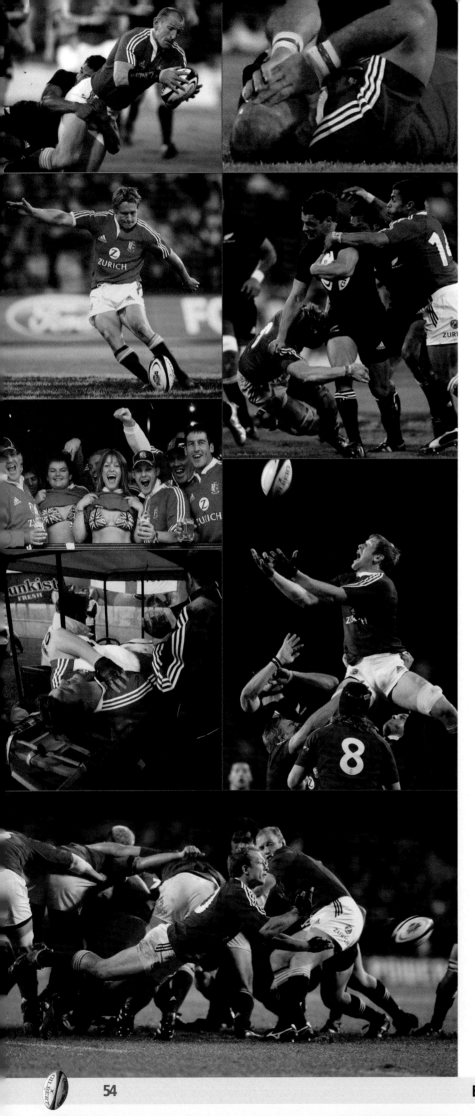

midfield marriage made in heaven lasted just 45 seconds of the first test as O'Driscoll's tour came to an abrupt halt at the hands of Tana Umaga and Kevin Mealamu. And World Cup-winning flanker Richard Hill was to go the same way as O'Driscoll with another knee injury sustained putting in one of his trademark tackles. Throw in the wind and torrential rain and it really was the blackest of nights in Christchurch as the Lions went down 21-3. "There have been times when I've had to fight back the tears," a sombre O'Driscoll reflected.

The so-called 'Midweek Massive' provided temporary respite as Shane Williams helped himself to a five-try blitz on one wing, while Jason Robinson delivered his first try since January 2 in the 109-6 rout of second division Manawatu. Sale Sharks colleague Hodgson continued to impress with a try in a 19-point personal haul.

Woodward then made an unprecedented 11 changes for the second test, with Lewis Moody stepping into a revamped back row and Jonny Wilkinson replacing Wales' Stephen Jones at fly half as the Lions tried to keep the series alive. At first the changes seemed to work. New skipper Gareth Thomas went over for a second minute try which Wilkinson duly converted to send the fans into raptures and the Lions into a 7-0 lead.

But New Zealand, whose play was wonderfully orchestrated by Daniel Carter, went on to dictate the pace and pattern of the game, turning in a flawless display on their way to a 48-18 win. The Lions had improved from the previous week, but New Zealand's superiority was still very much in evidence, despite Moody's defiant assertion that "this (New Zealand) team is beatable."

The final test side virtually selected itself with the Lions experiencing an ever-expanding injury list. Woodward made just three changes for the Auckland finale. England winger Mark Cueto, overlooked in the previous tests, made the side on the right wing after another impressive showing against Auckland. But the Sale Sharks' flyer found that he had little opportunity to shine in the match as the All Blacks again proved much too strong for the Lions.

Graham Henry's amazing side, who found themselves behind to two Stephen Jones penalties and down to 14 men when Umaga was sin-binned, somehow managed to strike back with two converted tries, before Umaga's subsequent brace either side of half time put the game beyond the Lions.

Moody's well-worked rumble over the line for a Lions try in the second period proved little consolation and appropriately it was the All Blacks who showed they still had enough time to find yet another gear – Rico Gear – as the Canterbury sensation confirmed the All Blacks' dominance with a try in the final act of the series to seal a 38-19 win and a convincing series 'Blackwash'.

ENGLAND'S LIONS

...And How They Performed

▼**Neil Back: Wellington (80 minutes played), NZ 1st Test (80), Manawatu (39, 1 Try) 199 total minutes played, 5 points scored**
Suspension prevented Back from appearing until four games into the tour. The 36 year old looked as fresh as ever against Wellington, but found life difficult in the opening test and disappeared from Woodward's plans.

▲**Mark Cueto: Bay Of Plenty (80, 1T), Southland (80), Manawatu (28★, 2T), Auckland (80), NZ 3rd Test (80) 348, 15**
Did nothing wrong all tour, but didn't see as much action as some expected. His weaving run against Auckland, which set up a Martyn Williams try, finally saw him get his chance in the third test.

▼**Martin Corry: Taranaki (80, 1T), Wellington (80), NZ 1st Test (80), Manawatu (80, 1T), NZ 2nd Test (1★ Sub), Auckland (25), NZ 3rd Test (13★) 359, 10**
Scored the try that proved the turning point in the Lions win over Taranaki. Deservedly named in the first test team and put in a committed display in difficult circumstances after taking over the captaincy from Brian O'Driscoll. Only made the bench for the following two tests.

▲**Lawrence Dallaglio: Bay Of Plenty (25) 25, 0**
Dallaglio, one of Woodward's chief Lionhearts, was in the shape of his life as he embarked on one last international crusade. But an awkward fall early on in the opening match against Bay Of Plenty resulted in a tour-ending broken ankle. "I've been around long enough to know that injuries are part of the game and no matter how difficult it is, you have to be philosophical. Now I just have to prepare myself mentally for the long process of recovery," he said.

▼**Matt Dawson: Bay Of Plenty (2★), NZ Maori (80), Otago (14★), NZ 1st Test (2★), Auckland (80), NZ 3rd Test (31★) 209, 0**
Played second fiddle to the excellent Dwayne Peel, but was always up for the fight when called upon.

▼**Will Greenwood: Taranaki (80), Otago (80, 1T), NZ 1st Test (77★), Auckland (50), NZ 3rd Test (80) 367, 5**
Still has an excellent rugby brain, but Greenwood found himself on the fringes for much of the tour. Started in the final test.

▲**Danny Grewcock: Taranaki (80), Wellington (80), Otago (14★), NZ 1st Test (22★) 196, 0**

Grewcock found himself on the wrong side of the law in New Zealand, resulting in him spending more time attending a disciplinary hearing than out on the pitch. An eight-hour IRB tribunal in Christchurch decided the Bath lock was guilty of biting All Blacks hooker Kevin Mealamu and he was suspended for two months.

▲**Richard Hill: Bay Of Plenty (80), NZ Maori (80), NZ 1st Test (23) 183, 0**

Hill brought off a fine tackle on Ali Williams in the 23rd minute of the opening test, but suffered damage to the medial ligament of the left knee that required reconstruction last October. The Saracens flanker, who spent six months on the sidelines, looks set for another long spell of rehabilitation.

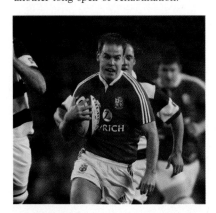

▲**Charlie Hodgson: Taranaki (80, 2C, 4P), Otago (75, 3C, 3P), Manawatu (50, 1T, 7C), Auckland (20, 1P) 225, 53**

A player who definitely enhanced his reputation on tour. Hodgson would definitely have been guaranteed a bench place in the final test had concussion not ruled him out.

▼**Ben Kay: Bay Of Plenty (80), Wellington (80), NZ 1st Test (58), Auckland (36) 254, 0**

An overhaul of the Lions' lineout calls in the week leading up to the opening test didn't work as well as anticipated against the All Blacks and Kay found it tough in the game despite giving his all. After this difficult test baptism he went on to play just 36 more minutes on the tour.

▼**Josh Lewsey: Bay Of Plenty (80, 2T), Maori (80), Wellington (69), NZ 1st Test (80), NZ 2nd Test (80), NZ 3rd Test 469, 10**

Mr. Consistency. Lewsey showed his finishing prowess with a brace of tries in the opening game, but had few opportunities thereafter. Effort and application were, of course, never lacking.

▼**Lewis Moody: Taranaki (80), Southland (80), NZ 2nd Test (80), NZ 3rd Test (74, 1T) 314, 5**

A definite success. Moody's aggressive approach proved a huge asset to the Lions back row in the final two tests and the Leicester Tigers man thoroughly deserved his try in the last game in Auckland.

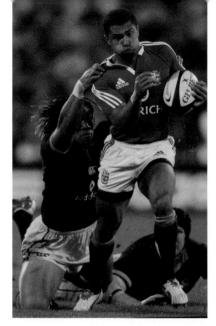

▲**Jason Robinson: Wellington (80), NZ 1st Test (58), Manawatu (58), NZ 2nd Test (80) 276, 5**

A late arrival, Robinson defended heroically in the first test but lost his place for the final test. The end of his 17-match try scoring drought – albeit against Manawatu – was a positive.

▲**Graham Rowntree: Taranaki (80), Otago (66), NZ 2nd Test (5★), Auckland (80), NZ 3rd Test (31★) 262, 0**

Rowntree was unlucky in that his main loosehead rivals – Gethin Jenkins and Andrew Sheridan – were two of the top performers in New Zealand. He still managed to appear off the bench in two tests, though, including the finale in Auckland after being cleared of foul play in the provincial game four days earlier.

▼Simon Shaw: NZ Maori (80), Otago (66), Southland (80), Manawatu (80), Auckland (80) 386, 0

Shaw, a late replacement for Malcolm O'Kelly, put in a series of strong displays that suggested he was unlucky not have been on the plane in the first place.

▼Andrew Sheridan: Bay Of Plenty (14*), NZ Maori (50), Otago (14*), Southland (39*), Manawatu (80) 197, 0

The England man mountain scored a clear points victory over formidable All Blacks tight-head Carl Hayman in the 19-13 defeat to the New Zealand Maori. However, replacement loosehead Gethin Jenkins went on to make the test spot his own. A leg injury disrupted the latter stages of Sheridan's tour.

▼Ollie Smith: Taranaki (80), Otago (24*), Southland (50), Manawatu (80, 1T) 234, 5

A niggling groin injury and later bruising to his ribs prevented Smith getting the test call-up that his brief but polished performances in the provincial matches perhaps deserved.

▲Matt Stevens: Bay Of Plenty (66), Wellington (3*), Otago (80), Southland (41), Manawatu (20*), Auckland (20*) 230, 0

Enjoyed a tour that will give him vital experience in years to come.

▲Andy Titterrell: Taranaki (70), Southland (51), Manawatu (39*) 160, 0

Made some decent hits in his first appearance against Taranaki, but the hooker found it tough with three other hookers contesting places.

▲Steve Thompson: Bay Of Plenty (14*), NZ Maori (75), Otago (14*), NZ 1st Test (22*), NZ 2nd Test (80) 205, 0

Had a tough time against the New Zealand Maori, but came back to make the Lions side for the second test. He deserves credit for the way he bounced back before going down with a viral illness on the eve of the last test.

▲Julian White: NZ Maori (80), Wellington (77), NZ 1st Test (80), NZ 2nd Test (75), NZ 3rd Test (80) 392, 0

White started all three tests and his destructive scrummaging kept England's front row in the contest throughout.

▼Jonny Wilkinson: Wellington (80, 2C, 3P), NZ 1st Test (80, 1P), NZ 2nd Test (66, 1C, 2P) 226, 24

Tackled himself to a standstill in his two t est appearances, which ultimately proved to be his undoing. Distributed the ball well, but found himself unable to stamp his authority on a tour which came to a premature end thanks to a 'stinger' injury.

HIGH IMPACT COLD THERAPY FOR SPORTS INJURIES

FREEZE PAIN INSTANTLY WITH DEEP FREEZE SPRAY. MAXIMISE MASSAGE AFTERWARDS WITH LONGER LASTING DEEP FREEZE COLD GEL.

ALWAYS READ THE LABEL. CONTAINS MENTHOL.

ENGLAND PLAYER BIOGRAPHIES

All the information you need on key players in
Andy Robinson's England set-up

STUART ABBOTT MBE

FAST FACTS

CLUB	**London Wasps**
POSITION	**Centre**
BORN	**3.6.78 Cape Town, South Africa**
HEIGHT	**1.83m**
WEIGHT	**89kg**
CAPS	**7**
POINTS	**10 – 2t**

Stuart Abbott scored on his England debut when he touched down one of the five tries in England's 43-9 Investec Challenge World Cup warm up match with Wales at the Millennium Stadium in August 2003. He went on to appear in three Rugby World Cup games, adding a second try in the runaway win over Uruguay. He rocketed to prominence in 2002-03 as a prime force in the London Wasps team that won the Zurich Premiership and was a deadly attacker in his club's brilliant run in season 2003-04, when they won the Heineken Cup and the Zurich Championship, one of the finest achievements in the history of English rugby. Born in South Africa to an English mother, he grew up in Cape Province where he was educated at the Diocesan College, a prep school also attended by Fraser Waters, a fellow centre at London Wasps. Abbott went on to the famous Stellenbosch University and played for Western Stormers as well as winning a South African U23 cap before joining London Wasps in November 2001. He was selected for England's 2003 summer tour of New Zealand and Australia, missed out on the 2004 RBS 6 Nations through injury, but was then called up for the 2004 summer tour where he came off the bench to replace Mike Catt in the first test against New Zealand in Dunedin. Although he earned a starting position in the second test in Auckland, Stuart had to be replaced by Fraser Waters because of an injury to his left shoulder. He was flown home for treatment and missed a good deal of the first half of the 2004-05 season, returning to the Wasps side in December 2004. Just nine games later and back to top form with his clever footwork and acceleration off the mark, in January 2005 he broke his leg in Wasps' Heineken Cup defeat against Biarritz, denying him selection for the RBS 6 Nations. The injury meant Abbot played just three games all season.

International Record
2003 W, F (3), RWC Sam, U, W (R), 2004 NZ (1R,2)

DID YOU KNOW?

Stuart became the eighth South African-born player to win a full cap for England when he played against Wales in the 2003 World Cup warm-up match. He took up the sport aged eight at Western Province Preparatory School in South Africa where rugby was compulsory. Phillipe Sella is one of his sporting heroes for his talent on the pitch, while All Black Tana Umaga counts as a particularly tough opponent for his "great all round game, strong in defence and attack." Away from rugby Stuart likes to lose himself with a Playstation and his DVDs. He's also a big fan of waterskiing.

IAIN BALSHAW MBE

FAST FACTS

CLUB	**Leeds Tykes**
POSITION	**Full back**
BORN	**14.4.79 Blackburn**
HEIGHT	**1.83m**
WEIGHT	**88kg**
CAPS	**24**
POINTS	**60 – 12t**

Iain Robert Balshaw is one of 19 England players who took the field during the 2003 World Cup final win over Australia in Sydney. He appeared as a replacement in extra time. Balshaw burst onto the international scene in 2000 when he was heralded as one of England's most exciting young talents. He was picked on the replacements' bench for every one of that year's internationals and finally made the starting line-up against Wales in the opening match of 2001. His startling performances in a heady 2001 Six Nations earned him a place on the 2001 Lions tour, although he didn't find his best form on the trip and didn't start in the test matches. However, the 2002-03 season saw him back to his best. He scored two tries in a 'non cap' international against Japan in Tokyo in June 2002, having recovered from shoulder surgery that restricted him to just nine games in the previous 11 months for Bath. Earlier that summer he had been a member of the England squad for the tour of New Zealand and Australia, before joining the party for Churchill Cup matches in North America. He bridged an 18-month gap between full test matches when playing in the World Cup warm-up match against France in Marseille. His pace and attacking verve saw him impress in England's World Cup game against Samoa, a match decided when he caught a diagonal kick from Jonny Wilkinson to score a try in the 70th minute. 'Balsh' had seemingly shaken off his continuing injury problems by the 2004 RBS 6 Nations, but fate took a hand again in the match against Ireland. A groin injury kept him out of serious action until this season, by which time he'd joined Leeds Tykes, making his debut for his new club in October 2004. At Leeds Balshaw enjoyed a revival in fortunes that saw him return to the international scene with a try-scoring performance against Italy in the 2005 RBS 6 Nations. He also played against Scotland and earned a place on the Lions tour to New Zealand. Unfortunately, an injury sustained in the Powergen Cup final against Bath meant Balshaw had to pull out of the trip to New Zealand before the squad had even left and was replaced by Mark Cueto.

International Record
2000 I(R), F(R), It(R), S(R), A(R), Arg, SA(R) 2001 W, It, S, F, I 2002 S(R), I(R) 2003 F (2&3) RWC Sam, U, A(R) 2004 It, S, I, 2005 It, S Lions: 2001 A(1R, 2R, 3R)

DID YOU KNOW?

Educated at Stonyhurst College, Balsh also played cricket and tennis for Lancashire at junior level. His first sporting success was his selection for Lancashire Under 15s at rugby. Former Bath and England player Mike Catt has influenced his rugby development, along with Jeremy Guscott. He enjoys playing golf and he would like to meet Tiger Woods one day. His first child, named Hope, was born in October 2004.

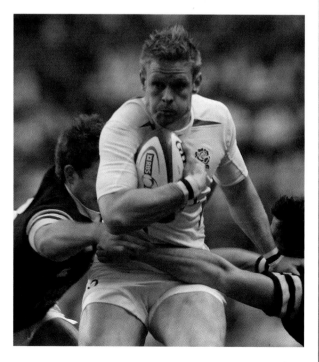

OLLY BARKLEY

FAST FACTS

CLUB	**Bath**
POSITION	**Fly half/Centre**
BORN	**28.11.81 Hammersmith**
HEIGHT	**1.78m**
WEIGHT	**92kg**
CAPS	**12**
POINTS	**32 – 1t, 3c, 7p**

Oliver Barkley will partly be known as the first player to win a full England cap without having played a game at senior club level in England. He achieved this distinction during England's summer tour to North America in 2001 when, having been called back from a stint with the Marist club in Christchurch, he came on as second half replacement in the 48-19 win against the USA Eagles. However, he really made his mark in the senior England squad during the 2004 RBS 6 Nations against Wales at Twickenham when he replaced an injured Paul Grayson at fly half. This debut as a starter came with just 24 hours notice and he delivered a very respectable 16 points. History repeated itself against France when Grayson's injury recurred and Olly started at the Stade de France. Again he delivered under pressure, though on that occasion he couldn't stop England slipping to defeat. His 2004 summer tour experience was also positive. He came off the bench in Auckland to replace injured centre Mike Tindall and was highly impressive.

Barkley was born in London, but was brought up in Cornwall. He attended Wadebridge Comprehensive and played for Wadebridge Camels before going on to the famous Bristol-based Colston's Collegiate. Here he played in two successive Daily Mail U18 Schools Cup winning sides, in 1999 and 2000 (as captain). He was instrumental in helping Bath top the 2003/04 Zurich Premiership and in May 2004 was voted Young Player of the Year by the Professional Rugby Players Association and won the Zurich Premiership Young Player of the Season award. While again producing the goods for Bath as they reached a cup final and fourth place in the Premiership, Barkley started on the bench in the game against Wales in 2005's RBS 6 Nations. Following that game he went on to start the four remaining matches at centre and even managed to score a try in the Twickenham defeat to France.

International Record
2001 USA (R) 2004 It (R), I (R), W, F, NZ (2R), A (R) 2005 W (R), F, I, It, S

DID YOU KNOW?

Olly is something of an all-rounder when it comes to sport. He had football trials for Plymouth Argyle and was also offered a trial with Arsenal, but preferred to play basketball. He probably would never have taken up rugby, but for a calculating PE teacher at Wadebridge School who insisted that he had to play the game if he also wanted to play football. He remains grateful to Wadebridge Camels coach, Cy Parry, along with Colston Collegiate's rugby master, Alan Martinovich, whom he describes as 'a fantastic coach and adviser'. Early career highlights include his first cap against the USA and beating Leeds Tykes to prevent Bath's relegation during the 2002/3 Zurich Premiership season. Outside rugby he surfs, plays table tennis to relax and is a fan of Radio 1.

ANDY BEATTIE

FAST FACTS

CLUB	Bath
POSITION	Flanker/Lock
BORN	6.9.78 London
HEIGHT	1.96m
WEIGHT	118kg
CAPS	Uncapped

Andy was a relatively late arrival on the international scene, having broken into the England A team for their match with France during the 2003-04 season at the age of 25. It was just reward for the burly back rower from London, who put in some exemplary performances for Bath, particularly alongside Michael Lipman and Zac Feaunati. 'Beastie', as he's known to his friends, has gone from young buck to senior pro in a very short space of time. An excellent ball carrier, he was also one of the Zurich Premiership's leading ball stealers at the lineout in the 2003-04 season. He is now seen by some as the outstanding blind-side flanker in the English Premiership. His playing career started with Richmond as a seven-year-old mini and he stayed with the club until taking up a Sports Science Degree course at Exeter University. Andy played in the same Hampton School team as the current England Sevens captain and Gloucester player Simon Amor. During his time at Hampton School he played for the England U18 Group Schools team and was on the unbeaten 1997 tour to Australia along with the likes of Mike Tindall, Steve Borthwick and Jonny Wilkinson. He also played for the South East U18s and U21s, the England U19 team and for the England U21 side that took park in the 1998 SANZAR tournament. During his time at university he played for Exeter Chiefs and led Exeter University to victory in the 2000 BUSA final. He moved to Bath in 2001, having gained a BSc Honours degree. He was ever present in their 2003-04 Zurich Premiership campaign, which culminated in a place in the Championship final when Bath lost to London Wasps at Twickenham. He prefers to play in the back row, but he also has the power and strength to play lock. Andy plays with his heart on his sleeve and was elevated to Bath captain during the absence of regular skipper Jonathan Humphreys in 2004/2005. However, with his early form earning him many plaudits, injury meant his season came to a premature end in February of this year.

DID YOU KNOW?

Andy says that being selected for England A is one of his treasured rugby memories, as was his first Premiership start with Bath, despite a 10-6 away defeat to Leeds Tykes. Playing at Twickenham in the 2004 Zurich Premiership Championship final is also high on his list, though he was again on the losing side. He says he owes a lot to his parents for their support, along with the help he received from Hampton School sports master Steve Timms. Dean Richards and Mike Teague were early inspirations, while now he has admiration for many of his Bath teammates including Danny Grewcock and Steve Borthwick. He feels indebted to forwards coach Mike Foley for the progress he has made under his guidance. To relax he enjoys a game of golf. As a child he was a member of the Royal Mid-Surrey Golf Club in Richmond.

CHRIS BELL

FAST FACTS

CLUB:	Leeds Tykes
POSITION:	Centre
BORN:	07.01.83 Plymouth
HEIGHT:	1.89m
WEIGHT:	100kg
CAPS:	Uncapped

Moving to Leeds Tykes from NEC Harlequins on a two-year contract at the end of the 2003-04 season, Chris Bell was able to renew his contact with coach Jon Callard after their successful working partnership with England U21s. An impressive, dashing centre and prolific try scorer, he became one of Tykes' top performers of the 2004-05 season. The first of many tries came against Sale Sharks and he also grabbed first half touchdowns in both the semi-final and the Twickenham final of the Powergen Cup as Tykes roared to victory over Bath in April 2005.

Having worked his way through the England Schools U16/U18 sides and the England U19 team, he became an important member of England's first ever U21 Grand Slam winning squad in 2004, playing in all five matches and scoring crucial tries against Ireland and France. He followed that up with a vital role in England U21s World Championships in Scotland 2004, making a try scoring appearance as captain against Argentina and also crossing against Wales. In his two years for England U21s, he played 16 times, all of them starts. He was called up to the England A team in 2005 for the one-off international against France A at Bath, winning 30-20. Chris was NEC Harlequins Young Player of the Year in the 2001-02 season, having joined them from his native Plymouth. Chris was nominated for his outstanding performances by Zurich in the 2004-05 Premiership season, was nominated for the PRA Young Player of the Year award and played a central role in the 2005 Churchill Cup.

DID YOU KNOW?

Both Chris' father, Dave, and his grandfather played for Wigan rugby league club and so it's not surprising that Chris has always been a fan of the alternative code. He started playing rugby union at the age of six with the Ivybridge club and was originally a prop because of his big shoulders, before becoming a fly half and, eventually, a centre. At NEC Harlequins he played alongside England centre Will Greenwood, who taught him a lot in the process. Another player whom he greatly admires is former Australian centre Tim Horan who he's played against on several occasions. His father has been a big influence on his career, as has his former Ivybridge Community College sports coach Malcolm Collins. He enjoys surfing, although it's not an easy interest to pursue, having recently lived in London and Leeds.

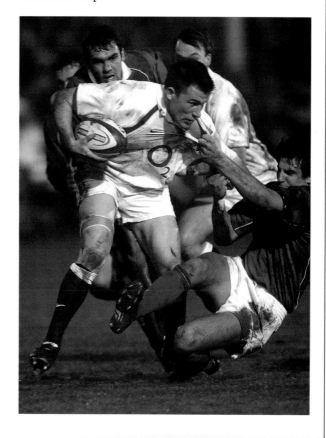

STEVE BORTHWICK

FAST FACTS

CLUB:	**Bath**
POSITION:	**Lock**
BORN:	**12.10.79 Carlisle**
HEIGHT:	**1.98m**
WEIGHT:	**111kg**
CAPS:	**19**
POINTS:	**0**

S tephen William Borthwick, who started in all three of England's tests in the Investec Challenge series in 2004, is recognised as one of the best lineout technicians in the English game. He established himself on the national stage after joining Bath from Preston Grasshoppers. A member of England's preliminary World Cup squad in 2003, he narrowly missed selection for the final 30. He had been a regular choice as the England A team captain from his debut against Wales A at

Wrexham in February 2001, though at the time he had already excelled on the full tour of South Africa the previous summer, where his dedication had impressed everyone. Injury prevented him being considered for the subsequent trip to Argentina the following year. Steve had a frustrating start in the RBS 6 Nations in 2004, being unavailable for selection for the first two games because of a disciplinary issue, before starting against Ireland at Twickenham as lock. He played against the All Blacks in Dunedin in the summer of 2004 after arriving as a replacement and started for his country both in the second test in Auckland and against the Wallabies in Brisbane. Borthwick was on the bench for all five Six Nations matches in 2005, making it onto the field on three occasions. Injury prevented Steve from taking part in the 2005 Churchill Cup.

International Record
2001 F, C (1, 2R), USA, Ro, 2003 A (R),W (2R), F (2) 2004 I, F (R) NZ (1R, 2) A 2004 C, SA, A 2005 W (R), It (R), S (R)

DID YOU KNOW?

Steve would probably have ended up working in the financial or insurance industry had he not become a professional rugby player. He graduated from Bath University in 2003 with a degree in Economics and Politics that took him five years to achieve, balancing it with his rugby commitments. He always wanted to play professional football when younger, but his secondary school played rugby and he became hooked. He made his Bath debut against Saracens in December 1998 and some of his former Bath colleagues – Martin Haag, Ollie Redman and Ben Clarke – were his early inspirations. He enjoys reading autobiographies.

ALEX BROWN

FAST FACTS

CLUB	**Gloucester**
POSITION	**Lock**
BORN	**17/05/79 Bristol**
HEIGHT	**2.01m**
WEIGHT	**110kg**
CAPS	**Uncapped**

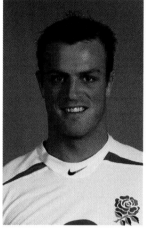

Alex is a tall, agile, lock and an excellent lineout jumper who also contributes immensely in the loose. His work in winning ball against the throw is a real strength and has been much in evidence for Gloucester since his move to Kingsholm from Bristol in the summer of 2003. At Gloucester he was top of the league line out statistics during his first season, 2003-04. Born in Bristol, his career began as a mini with Clifton and by the time he left that club, he had played for the South West U18s, the England Colts team and, in 1998/99, the England U21s. He was a member of the 1999 SANZAR tournament squad that played in New Zealand. Like Olly Barkley his skills were honed at Bristol's Colston's Collegiate under Alan Martinovich and Andy Robinson (now England Head Coach) and that association led to a year's contract at Bath. Six months into it, he went on loan to Pontypool and stayed with the Welsh club for 18 months. Alex then joined his native team, Bristol, and under Dean Ryan's guidance became Player of the Year in the

2001-02 season and made a forceful second row partnership with Garath Archer. He joined Gloucester for the 2003/04 season, where he again linked up with his former Shoguns coach Dean Ryan and enjoyed a spectacular debut season. He made his England A debut in 2002 against Scotland and was also a member of the England squad that won the Churchill Cup in Canada in 2003, returning to North America for the 2004 tour. Alex played for the England XV against the Barbarians in May 2003 in a non-capped game and again in the same fixture one year later. He was injured just before the 2004 Investec Challenge autumn internationals, but made his return for Gloucester in the New Year. In May 2004 his try against Leicester Tigers was voted Zurich Premiership Try Of The Season. Injury has unfortunately dogged Alex this year and he missed part of the last season, but nevertheless managed to rack up 18 appearances for Gloucester.

DID YOU KNOW?

Alex's father Peter also played in the second row for Bristol before moving to Clifton. At 6'7" Alex has the edge with a three-inch height advantage over his dad! A proud Bristolian, he freely admits that he would love to be playing for Bristol Shoguns to this day and that it was one of the worst moments in his rugby career when they were relegated at the end of the 2002/03 season. Alex likes fast cars and watching F1 racing. He owned a growling TVR when he played for Bristol and he's currently renovating a property in the city, which offers him a break away from rugby.

GEORGE CHUTER

FAST FACTS

CLUB	Leicester Tigers
POSITION	Hooker
BORN	09.07.76 Greenwich
HEIGHT	1.78m
WEIGHT	100kg
CAPS	Uncapped

George first started playing as a 12 year old when he went to Trinity School in Croydon. He quickly established himself at hooker and has played there ever since. He went on to play his club rugby for Old Mid-Whitgiftians and gained representative honours for the London Division U18 side. In 1994-95 he won his first international cap for England Colts against Scotland and also went on that year's summer tour to Canada. He was invited to trial for Saracens at the age of 19 and stayed with them for five years. In 1998 he made a try-scoring debut for England A against France A at Tours and in the same year went on the senior England 'tour to hell' to Australia, New Zealand and South Africa, featuring in the uncapped match at Invercargill against New Zealand Academy. George took a year off, then joined Leicester Tigers in December 2000 and, after the departure of Richard Cockerill in the summer of 2002, vied with Dorian West as first choice hooker. In 2003 he was back in the England reckoning and in 2004 was a member of the England Churchill Cup squad in Canada. Following that tour he was selected for the Elite Player Squad, but a second citing in October resulted in him missing the opportunity to take part in the November tests.

DID YOU KNOW?

The young Chuter was far more interested in cricket, played as an all rounder for the local school sides and was watched by Surrey for a time. It wasn't until he was 15 that, having played rugby for the London Schools and Surrey, he suddenly realised that he had probably found his metier. He went to Brunel University where he had a career in teaching in mind, but after a year he packed it in and joined Saracens as a professional. When his four-year contract came to an end, he decided to travel in the USA and Australia and he was in Sydney for the 2000 Olympic Games. On returning he signed for Leicester Tigers in December 2000 where his childhood role model Dean Richards was in charge, and at a time when Tigers were in the middle of their first European Cup-winning season. George sees his highlights to date as winning the Tetley Cup in 1998 with Saracens, and the Tigers game against Leinster this year in Dublin. To relax he enjoys golf but, in truth, is a real family man and likes nothing better than spending time with wife Katy and their two daughters, Ellie and Georgia.

BEN COHEN MBE

FAST FACTS

CLUB:	**Northampton Saints**
POSITION:	**Wing/Centre**
BORN:	**14.9.78 Northampton**
HEIGHT:	**1.87m**
WEIGHT:	**100kg**
CAPS:	**46**
POINTS:	**145 – 29t**

Ben Cohen appeared as a replacement in two of England's 2004 autumn internationals and was showing fine form again for Northampton Saints by the turn of the year, often playing in the centre. At the time of the 2003 Rugby World Cup Cohen had established himself as one of the great wings in world rugby. He started in all but one of England's matches and his part in England's triumph against Australia in the final game marked a unique family double. George Cohen, Ben's uncle, was at right back when England won the World Cup football final in 1966. Ben has always had pace to spare, but his power is also a key factor. Ireland found this out to their cost in 2000 when he ran in two tries on his international debut.

Ben first took up the game aged 12 at Northampton Old Scouts. He was educated at Kingsthorpe Upper School, Northampton and joined the Scouts after seeing details of the Club on his school notice board. A year after his England debut, he was chosen for the 2001 Lions, and although he didn't figure in the test series he did manage to score twice in the match against New South Wales Country Cockatoos at Coffs Harbour. He played in every one of England's matches in the 2002-3 season, scoring a spectacular try against the All Blacks, and he also notched twice against the Australians during the Investec Challenge series at Twickenham. One of his most memorable tries was scored against Australia in June 2003 as England swept aside the host nation by 25-14 to complete their southern hemisphere tour unbeaten. It's not just southern hemisphere games that Ben relishes, though – in the 2004 RBS 6 Nations he was named man of the match against Wales, partly for two striking tries. This season has been tough for him as Saints battled against relegation all season. He suffered an injury in the North v South Tsunami match and the form of Mark Cueto also kept Cohen's Six Nations appearances down to just one replacement appearance against France.

International Record
2000 I, F, W, It, S, SA (2), Arg, SA 2001 W, It, S, F, Ro 2002 S, I, F, W, It, NZ, A, SA 2003 W, S, I, NZ, A, F (1,2&3), RWC G, SA, Sam, W, F, A 2004 It, S, I, W, F NZ (1& 2) A, C (R) SA (R) 2005 F (R) Lions: 2001

DID YOU KNOW?

Ben's Uncle George, England's football World Cup winner, remains his sporting hero. Ben believes that the footballing heroes of 1966 still don't get the recognition they truly deserve. Before his successful Rugby World Cup, Ben had many career highlights. He played for Northampton in their Heineken Cup triumph in 2000 and was part of the England Grand Slam team in 2003. He owns several beautiful motorbikes, including an American touring bike, and had he not become a professional player, Ben is convinced he would have become a fireman or policeman.

MARTIN
CORRY MBE

FAST FACTS

CLUB	**Leicester Tigers**
POSITION	**No 8/Flanker**
BORN	**12.10.73 Birmingham**
HEIGHT	**1.95m**
WEIGHT	**114kg**
CAPS	**37**
POINTS	**15 – 3t**

Martin Edward Corry burst back into the limelight with outstanding performances in each of the three Investec Challenge matches in the autumn of 2004, especially with a brilliant game against South Africa. He has been one of Leicester Tigers' core forwards for several seasons and demonstrated this to full effect in the two Heineken Cup matches against London Wasps in December 2004. He first played for England in 1997 and came to prominence with startling performances after arriving as a replacement on the 2001 Lions tour of Australia, where he appeared in all three test matches. He was educated at Tunbridge Wells Grammar School and the University of Northumbria and first played rugby for Tunbridge Wells minis before joining Newcastle Falcons, Bristol Shoguns, then finally Leicester Tigers. During his career he has worked his way up the full representative ladder, turning out for England at Schools, Students, U21 and A level, as well as the 2001 Lions tour to Australia. He was called up after the tour had started due to an injury to Scotland's Simon Taylor and immediately impressed Graham Henry, the then Lions coach. He confirmed his selection for Clive Woodward's 2003 Rugby World Cup squad in a highly competitive back row area with a powerful late run in England's warm up matches – he was outstanding in the 43-9 defeat of Wales at the Millennium Stadium in late summer of 2003 and then again in the September defeat of France at Twickenham. Martin finally cemented his place in the England team during the 2005 RBS Six Nations, playing in four of the five matches and confirmed his status as having moved out of the shadow cast by Hill, Dallaglio and Back by captaining the side in Jason Robinson's absence against both Italy and Scotland. Not only that, but he also grabbed a try in the defeat to Ireland and was then named in the 2005 Lions squad from the beginning.

International Record
1997 Arg (1, 2) 1998 N, It, SA(R) 1999 F (R), A, C(R), World Cup It (R), NZ (R), SA (R) 2000 I (R), F (R), W (R), It (R), S (R), Arg (R), SA (R) 2001 W (R), It (R), F (R), C (1), I 2002 F (R), W (R) 2003 W, F (2&3), RWC U 2004 A (R) C, SA, A 2005 F, I, It, S Lions: 2001 A (1, 2, 3) Lions: 2005 NZ (1, 2R, 3R)

DID YOU KNOW?

During the 2003 Rugby World Cup 'Cozza' flew home from Australia to attend the birth of his first child, a daughter called Eve. He rejoined the squad just days later. Playing for Leicester Tigers and England, it is not surprising that he chooses the former England captain Martin Johnson as his sporting hero, both for his leadership and for his playing qualities. He names Bath and England lock Danny Grewcock as his toughest opponent. Outside rugby, Martin would most like to meet Ed Moses and the Tour de France cyclist Lance Armstrong. Like his Tigers teammate Neil Back, Cozza admits to being "too tidy and organised. It can be irritating, I know". And he's none too fond of cats, which is rather ironic given the fact that his wife has two of them.

MARK CUETO

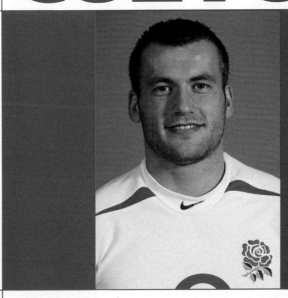

FAST FACTS

CLUB	Sale Sharks
POSITION	Wing
BORN	26.12.79
HEIGHT	1.83m
WEIGHT	93kg
CAPS	8
POINTS	40 – 8t

Mark Cueto announced himself on the test stage with four tries in his first three internationals after winning his first cap against Canada in November 2004. He started in all three autumn tests and his pace and finishing ability created a wonderful first impression. In fact, he scored on his Sale Sharks debut at Bristol and he's continued doing so with regularity ever since. He was the Zurich Premiership's top try scorer in 2002/03 with 13, the second highest behind club mate Steve Hanley in 2003/04 with 11, and he started 2004/05 with four in as many games. His rugby career kicked off with the Netherhall RFC minis but, aged eight, the family moved to Wolverhampton and he joined Dudley Kingswinford. Two years later they moved again to soccer mad Crewe, where he took up the round ball game as a left back or midfielder during his time at St.Thomas Moore Catholic High School and even represented South Cheshire at football. It wasn't until he was in the sixth form that he started to get properly interested in rugby once more and it was during a knockabout match that he was noticed by local schoolteacher Lyndsey Purcell, who wrote to Sale Sharks and got them to sign him. He completed a BSc in Sports Science at the local university and played for Altrincham Kersall before making his Sharks debut in 2001, aged 21. It was a big year for him, touring Argentina with England and playing for the England Sevens team. The following year he made his England A debut and has been on Churchill Cup tours in both 2003 and 2004. He also played for the England XV who took on the Barbarians at Twickenham in May 2003.

But all of this paled in comparison to a phenomenal 2005 RBS 6 Nations in which he was the top scorer with four tries,

making it eight tries in eight games for England. These performances have sealed Mark's position as one of Andy Robinson's key players. Despite being first choice winger for England, though, Cueto didn't make the initial British Lions squad for New Zealand, but was called up by Head Coach Sir Clive Woodward before the plane even left Heathrow due to Iain Balshaw's late withdrawal through injury and started in the final test.

International Record
2004 C, SA, A 2005 W, F, I, It, S Lions: 2005 NZ (3)

DID YOU KNOW?

Cueto is originally a Spanish name; Mark's great grandparents originated from that country. His debut for Sale Sharks and winning the Parker Pen Shield with them are two of his favourite rugby moments, but his England success in the Investec Challenge autumn internationals must now rank as his highlight so far. But there was a downside. Mark's phone bill after replying to all the good luck messages he got from friends and family came to a whopping £200! To unwind away from the game Mark likes nothing better than a game of golf, a film or a nice meal with long time girlfriend Amy.

MATT DAWSON MBE

FAST FACTS

CLUB	**London Wasps**
POSITION	**Scrum half**
BORN	**31.10.72 Birkenhead**
HEIGHT	**1.77m**
WEIGHT	**90kg**
CAPS	**70**
POINTS	**96 – 15t, 6c, 3pg**

Matthew James Sutherland Dawson is one of the finest scrum halves in the sport. He celebrated his 50th cap against Ireland when England won the Grand Slam in 2003 and earned his 60th against the same opposition one year on. He is England's most capped scrum half and played a critical role for his country in the 2003 World Cup, feeding Jonny Wilkinson for the fateful drop goal. A master of the quick 'tap and go' penalty, he has stretched the very best of defences over the years, both at international and club level. Educated at RGS High Wycombe, where he played alongside former England full back Nick Beal, he gained his first England cap in 1995. He toured with the Lions in 1997, playing all three tests against South Africa and scoring a famous try that turned the first test in Cape Town. He was also on the 2001 Lions tour to Australia. He stood in as England's captain when Martin Johnson was injured, leading the side on nine occasions and to the 2001 Six Nations crown. When called on he can also demonstrate his versatility by kicking goals. He learnt his early club rugby with Marlow, kept wicket for Buckinghamshire and played football for Chelsea Boys. His long career at Northampton Saints finished at the end of the 2003-04 season and he has since impressed playing for London Wasps. He left the Elite Player Squad in the autumn of 2004. But he was back in the fold in 2005. Matt started against Wales, and was then used as a substitute in the remaining four Six Nations games. He earned a call-up to the 2005 Lions squad.

International Record
1995 WS 1996 F, W, S, I 1997 A, SA, NZ (2) 1998 W (R), S, I, NZ (1, 2), SA, N, It, A, SA 1999 S, F (R), W, A (R), USA, C World Cup It, NZ, Tg, Fj (R), SA 2000 I, F, W, It, S, A (R), Arg, SA 2001 W, It, S, F, I 2002 W, It (R), NZ, A, SA 2003 It, S, I, A, F (3R), RWC G, Sam, W, F, A 2004 It (R), S (R), I, W, F NZ (1, 2R), A(R) 2005 W, F (R), (R), It (R), S (R)
Lions: 1997 SA (1, 2, 3), 2001 A (2R, 3), 2005 NZ (1R, 3R)

DID YOU KNOW?

Matt's father Ron encouraged him to take up rugby and coached him, greatly influencing his early development. His sporting hero when a youngster was Nick Farr-Jones of Australia and appropriately he describes the Australian World Cup captain George Gregan, his opposite number in the World Cup final, as "always a threat whatever, wherever." He says that the three people he'd most love to have round for dinner would be his granddad Sam, who sadly died when Matt was 14, Brad Pitt (for his girlfriend) and boxing legend Muhammad Ali.

LOUIS DEACON

FAST FACTS

CLUB	Leicester Tigers
POSITION	Lock
BORN	07.10.80
HEIGHT	1.98m
WEIGHT	116kg
CAPS	Uncapped

Louis Deacon joined Leicester Tigers in 2000 and having lived in the shadow of the England pairing of Martin Johnson and Ben Kay for several seasons, he grasped the opportunity in 2003-04 to command a regular place during the World Cup season. He made 23 appearances in all that season, and by the end he was being picked ahead of Kay. He made his first team debut in August 2000 as a replacement against Cardiff

and has established himself as a highly dependable player, equally at home at the front or middle of the lineout. His playing career started as an eight year old with Wigston, before joining Syston and, as a Ratcliffe College student, going on to represent the Midlands county and both the England 16 Group and U18 Group School sides. He joined the Leicester Tigers Academy in the 1997-98 season and worked his way through the Tigers Youth, U21 and Extras teams. Having already played for the England U21 side, he was called up to the England A squad in the 2002-03 season, but unfortunately sickness forced him to withdraw. From September 2003, along with his Leicester teammate Harry Ellis, he was also named in the RFU's Senior National Academy, part of the Elite Player Squad. Louis has just finished an impressive season with Tigers and played in their Zurich Premiership final defeat to London Wasps in May.

DID YOU KNOW?

Louis followed in his dad Paul's footsteps, playing in the second row at Wigston, the same club that nurtured England's World Cup winning captain and Leicester Tigers hero Martin Johnson. The Tigers captain has always been someone Louis has looked up to and tried to emulate since joining the Welford Road ranks straight from school. It was the same 2000 season in which Tigers won the European Cup and, although he didn't play in the final, he still rates the day as one of his favourite rugby memories. He was also a fine field athlete while at school and won an area title in the shot putt. Louis briefly enjoyed boxing and rates Muhammad Ali as one of his all time sporting icons.

HARRY ELLIS

FAST FACTS

CLUB	**Leicester Tigers**
POSITION	**Scrum half**
BORN	**17.05.82 Leicester**
HEIGHT	**1.78m**
WEIGHT	**89kg**
CAPS	**7**
POINTS	**5 – 1t**

Harry Alistair Ellis won his first England caps as a replacement, coming on in place of Andy Gomarsall in the Investec Challenge matches against South Africa and Australia in autumn 2004 and is seen as one of the most promising of England's new recruits. A Leicester man through and through, he was born in the city and started playing the game as a six year old with the South Leicester club. He studied at Leicester Grammar School, where he represented Leicester Schools and the Midlands at every age level, as well as the England A, U16 Group and U18 Group schools sides. In fact, he played for the England U18 side when he was only 16. Having spent a year with the Wigston, club he joined the Leicester Tigers Academy where he combined playing with further education at De Montfort University. He worked his way through the Tigers' lower teams and continued his representative career, playing for both the England U19 and U21 sides. He has also featured in the England Sevens squad along with his teammate Louis Deacon. He made his first team Tigers debut in 2001 and was named Tigers' Players Young Player of the Year for the 2001-02 season. He finally established himself as a regular in the No 9 spot during the 2003-04 season, making 19 appearances and helping Tigers bounce back from a poor start and a turbulent midseason to reach the Zurich Wild Card final. In 2005, along with the Tigers' resurgence as a force in English rugby, Ellis made the England No 9 shirt his own under stiff competition from rival Matt Dawson. He came on as a sub against Wales, but then started the four remaining Six Nations fixtures, culminating in his first try for England against Scotland.

International Record

2004 SA (R), A (R) 2005 W (R), F, I, It, S

DID YOU KNOW?

Harry is one of three rugby-playing brothers whose father, Bob Ellis, was a former Tigers back row player. In fact, Harry is the odd one out in the family as both elder brothers Mark and Robert were breakaway forwards. Harry says he gets a great kick pulling on the Tigers shirt every time they play. A self-confessed sports fiend, he likes watching all manner of sports, including boxing and cricket, and used to be a talented club freestyle swimmer. Harry is into extreme sports too, admitting he would love to go skydiving and bungee jumping and enjoys go-karting. He would also like to appear on the TV programme 'The Weakest Link'.

AYOOLA ERINLE

FAST FACTS

CLUB	**London Wasps**
POSITION	**Centre**
BORN	**20.02.80 Lagos, Nigeria**
HEIGHT	**1.93m**
WEIGHT	**106kgs**
CAPS	**Uncapped**

Ayoola, or 'Oogie' to his friends, is one of the biggest centres in the Guinness Premiership and is a dominant presence on the pitch against opposing defences who have the task of bringing down the 16 stoner when in full flight. Although born in Nigeria, he was brought to Britain when just 18 months old. His rugby career didn't flourish until he was nine when he started at the exclusive Oratory School on the outskirts of his home town, Reading. As the school was in Oxfordshire, his first representative rugby was for that county, before joining Reading at 15 and playing for Berkshire. He was also a member of The Oratory School team that reached the final of the Rosslyn Park tournament, but lost to Sherborne. His career really took off at 19 when he played for the England Students side in the World Cup in Italy. That year he also played for the England Sevens World Series team in Durban and in Dubai, where he was the joint leading try scorer. His London Wasps career, however, took a while to get going and after a loan period at Henley Hawks, he finally made his Premiership debut against Gloucester in the 2002-03 season. Although injury dogged him early on, he remained injury-free through 2004-05 to command a regular place in the team and start in Wasps successful Zurich Premiership final in May against Leicester Tigers. Ayoola was nominated for Zurich Player of the Season 2004-05. Ayoola marked Jonah Lomu in his comeback match at Twickenham.

DID YOU KNOW?

Ayoola, whose name means Joy of Wealth, didn't like rugby until he arrived at The Oratory School where it was compulsory and it grew on him after a couple of seasons. Since then the sport has enthused the whole family, as both his two eldest sisters Dami and Biniki play rugby as well as turning up with mother Titi, father Dapo, youngest sister Dieks and cousin Bimby for every match he plays. Coach Shaun Edwards and former Wasps Director of Rugby Warren Gatland have been hugely supportive in the last couple of seasons and have guided his career to date, which included playing in London Wasps 2004 Heineken Cup win. In his spare time, laid-back Ayoola is learning to play the piano and he's an active churchgoer. If he hadn't got the rugby bug he would probably have moved into a science or medical-based career, having attained As in A-Level Physics and Chemistry.

JAMES FORRESTER

FAST FACTS

CLUB	**Gloucester**
POSITION	**No 8/Back row**
BORN	**09.02.81 Oxford**
HEIGHT	**1.95m**
WEIGHT	**100kg**
CAPS	**1**
POINTS	**0**

James is a tall, agile, talented No 8 with excellent ball-handling skills and an eye for the try line, as his impressive tally for Gloucester demonstrates. Born in Oxford, he learnt his rugby at school and as a mini/junior with Bicester RFC. During his time at St. Edward's School, Oxford, he also developed his game and although disappointed at missing out on an England U18 Group Schools cap in 1999, he had more than made up for it by the end of that year when

he signed for Gloucester. Having played for England U21, he made his England A debut against Wales in Bristol during 2002 and in June of that year also played for an England XV against the Barbarians at Twickenham, scoring a memorable 65 metre try, outstripping Jonah Lomu in the process. He was also capped by the England sevens squad in 2002, playing in the opening World Series tournament in Durban and two others, and was 'Man of the Match' with two tries when England A thrashed Scotland 78-6 in March 2003. Unfortunately, injury has affected James' career and he required an elbow operation in 2002-03, then dislocated his shoulder in 2003-04 in the England A match against France. In the summer of 2004 he signed a three-year contract to stay at Kingsholm. This season he sneaked his first England cap, against Wales in the RBS 6 Nations, coming on as a blood replacement for Joe Worsley. James has shown his versatility, sometimes moving from No 8 to centre, which he did in Gloucester's defeat in May's Zurich Premiership wildcard final against Saracens. Forester was selected for the Churchill Cup in 2005.

International Record
2005 W (R)

DID YOU KNOW?

James' grandfather, David Naylor, captained Coventry and also played for Bath, while his dad also turned out for Oxford and Oxfordshire in the back row. However, he could have been persuaded to take up a career as a professional footballer during his time at Isis Middle School, when he was a promising centre back and had trials for Oxford United. Rugby prevailed while at St. Edward's, Oxford. James admired All Black Christian Cullen for his pace and strength along with Zinzan Brooke and England centre Jeremy Guscott. He has long been a Chelsea season ticket holder. His Twickenham appearances in the Powergen Cup final, the 2002 Zurich Championship final and playing for England against the Barbarians are his rugby highlights and one of his proudest moments came in 2003 when he was crowned Zurich Premiership Young Player of the Year. He likes travelling and just before turning professional, toured Asia, India, Nepal and Thailand for six months. James' motto in life is 'to give my best in everything I do.'

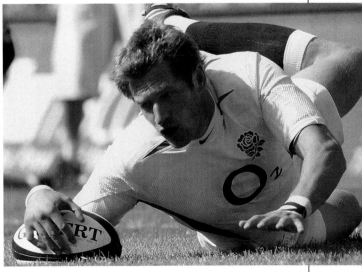

PERRY FRESHWATER

FAST FACTS

CLUB	**Perpignan**
POSITION	**Prop**
BORN	**27.07.73 Wellington, New Zealand**
HEIGHT	**1.83m**
WEIGHT	**110kg**
CAPS	**Uncapped**

Perry Thomas Freshwater, the son of a Walthamstow father, lived all his early life in New Zealand. He started playing rugby as a five year old for the Wellington club before going on to Wellington College, where he was first capped by the New Zealand Schoolboys against the touring Welsh Schoolboys in Christchurch in 1990. He also played for the New Zealand U19 and U21 teams before deciding to spend a year in England and to play for Leicester Tigers. He made his debut against Nottingham in 1995 and went on to make almost 100 appearances for Tigers, many of them off the bench, and became firm friends and flatmates with the then Tigers hooker Richard Cockerill. In 2004 he picked up his only England A cap when he played against France in Perpignan after joining the French club for the 2002-03 season. He was in the Perpignan team that lost to Stade Francais in that season's French Club Championship final, but they failed to repeat the experience in 2004-05. England have long had their eye on the prop and his first opportunity to impress on tour came in this year's successful Churchill Cup campaign where he started in both games and was named Vice Captain in the final.

DID YOU KNOW?

Now that he lives near the sea in the south of France, Perry swims most days of the year and is a wakeboarding specialist. His house in the Perpignan countryside is surrounded by a vineyard, complete with orchard. He likes to walk in the nearby Pyrenees or visit Barcelona, only a two-hour drive away. He enjoys cooking and specialises in local fresh seafood on his barbeque most evenings. He maintains the players of Leicester Tigers 'ABC club' taught him all there is to know about propping, particularly Richard Cockerill and Darren Garforth, and he describes their work ethic as incredible. He quickly settled in at Perpignan and thoroughly enjoys the physical nature of French rugby.

ANDY GOMARSALL MBE

FAST FACTS

CLUB	**Worcester Warriors**
POSITION	**Scrum half**
BORN	**24.7.74 Durham**
HEIGHT	**1.77m**
WEIGHT	**91kg**
CAPS	**23**
POINTS	**34 – 6t, 2c**

Andy Gomarsall started all three of England's 2004 Investec Challenge autumn internationals at Twickenham and was made vice captain for the England XV against the Barbarians in May as well as for the successful 2005 Churchill Cup tour. He leaves Gloucester to join Worcester Warriors next season, where he will be playing alongside the Warriors captain Pat Sanderson, who is also England's Churchill Cup captain. In 2002 'Gomars' re-ignited his England rugby career after a period of 27 months in the international wilderness when he played in the 26-18 win over Argentina in Buenos Aires. He continued the momentum in 2003 when he played in six tests, including the Rugby World Cup, scoring two tries in the 111-13 win over Uruguay in the pool match in Brisbane. Andy sprang to prominence when he led the 1992 England Schools U18 team to their first Grand Slam in 11 years. The following season he joined London Wasps and made his full England debut in 1996 against Italy. In 1997 he played in three Six Nations games and came on twice as a replacement on tour in Argentina. He is noted for massive application to his personal training programme and this dedication all came to fruition with his call up for the 2003 World Cup. He sealed his place as one of the three scrum halves for the World Cup with a fine performance in England's

43-9 defeat of Wales at the Millennium Stadium during the World Cup warm-up matches. Coming out of those World Cup performances, Gomars was selected as England vice captain for the non-cap game against the New Zealand Barbarians in December 2003. On the club scene, he was a member of London Wasps' 1999 Powergen Cup winning side, then transferred to Bedford, where he was captain, before opting to join Gloucester. He took part in his second Powergen Cup triumph with the cherry and whites in 2003. Worcester will welcome his experience in 2005/06. He was Vice Captain in the first Churchill Cup match and scored a try in the closing minutes of the final.

International Record

1996 It, Arg 1997 S, I, F, Arg (2R) 2000 It (R) 2002 Arg, SA (R) 2003 F, W (R), W, F (2R) RWC G (R), U 2004 It, S, NZ (1R, 2) A, C, SA, A

DID YOU KNOW?

Andy's father has been a strong influence on his game from an early age, even before his first sporting success when making the Doncaster Under-6 team. He believes Gareth Edwards was history's greatest scrum half. After he retires from playing rugby Andy sees himself moving into coaching.

ANDY GOODE

FAST FACTS

CLUB	Leicester Tigers
POSITION	Fly half
BORN	03.04.80 Coventry
HEIGHT	1.80m
WEIGHT	95kg
CAPS	2
POINTS	2

Andy was called onto the England bench against Ireland in this year's RBS 6 Nations but made his debut coming off the bench late into the second half of England's 39-7 victory over Italy, with just enough time to convert a late Andy Hazell try. Andy has hit top form since returning to Leicester Tigers in December 2003 after spending almost 18 months with London-based club Saracens. He is the leading points scorer in the Zurich Premiership for the past two seasons and ended the 2003-4 season with the unique distinction of being the top points scorer for both Tigers and

Saracens. In May 2004 his personal 30 point haul in the 75-13 victory over Rotherham included a Tigers league record of 10 successful conversions. During his first spell with Tigers he accrued two Heineken Cup winners' medals, an inaugural Zurich Championship medal and played a substantial part in the club's record four successive Premiership titles.

In 1998 Andy played for England U18 and has also represented England at U21 level, playing at the 2000 SANZAR tournament in New Zealand, as well as making five appearances for England A in 2001 and 2002. Andy was nominated for Zurich Player of the Season 2004-05 and the PRA Players' Player of the Year. He ended last season being voted Player of the Year by the Leicester Tigers players, then made a significant contribution to England's Churchill Cup success in Canada.

International Record 2005
It (R), S (R)

DID YOU KNOW?

Andy is an all-round sportsman and could have made it to the top in several sports. From 7 to 14 he was a top-class breaststroke swimmer, competing at the National Championships and often beating close rival Adam Whitehead, who later won Commonwealth Gold in 2002. From the age of 12 to 19 Andy captained the Warwickshire junior cricket teams as an opener and was offered a professional contract at 16, which he turned down. He studied at King Henry VIII School, Coventry, but started playing rugby at Barkers Butts at 5, before moving to Nuneaton at 12 and then Coventry aged 16, also playing for Warwickshire and the Midlands. 'Goodie' enjoys golf, playing off 10 and one of his best friends is Morgan Williams, Saracens and Canada scrum half.

PRACTICE MAKES JONNY.

A shot like that takes a lot of balls.
276,000 in fact - 1,000 practice kicks every
week of Jonny's professional career.
That's the kind of training that's made him
the most precise kicker in international
rugby. He doesn't take preparation lightly.
Including drinking Lucozade Sport
before every training session, not just
every game. Working closely with Jonny,
our scientists at the Lucozade Sport
Science Academy have found that fuelling
muscles before sport increases
endurance - making him train harder for
longer. So when match day comes,
a penalty kick from 60 yards won't be so
much of a long shot.

ARE YOU READY?

DANNY GREWCOCK MBE

FAST FACTS

CLUB	**Bath**
POSITION	**Lock**
BORN	**7.11.72 Coventry**
HEIGHT	**1.98m**
WEIGHT	**117kg**
CAPS	**57**
POINTS	**10 – 2t**

It's hard to imagine an England second row without Daniel Jonathan Grewcock now. After being a fixture in England's pack in the Investec Challenge games in Autumn 2004, starting in all three tests, Grewcock was a starter in all five RBS 6 Nations matches in 2005. Whereas he once struggled to break up the Kay/Johnson partnership, it's now a case of who's going to partner Grewcock. He deserves his day in the sun after bad luck at the 2003 Rugby World Cup when he was only able to make one appearance on the pitch after breaking a hand in the Uruguay match. He had already missed games in the competition due to a toe injury. His injuries left then Head Coach Clive Woodward with no choice but to replace Danny mid-competition and to fly out Simon Shaw. He finally received his World Cup medal in December 2004. The Bath stalwart is one of a group of talented players, along with the likes of Ben Kay, who have partnered former skipper Martin Johnson in the England boiler room. He is an accomplished lineout jumper, as the Lions recognised in 2001 when he played in all three test matches against the Wallabies and in six of the 10 tour matches. With the retirement of Johnson, Danny slipped effortlessly into the lock position for the 2004 RBS 6 Nations and emphatically justified selection with a stormer of a match against Scotland, scoring his second international try. Although injury prevented him from playing against Ireland, he made a strong return to the team against Wales and his early exit, again through injury, against France caused a loss of momentum. Danny's career started with Barkers Butts and Coventry and he was soon making a name for himself at the age of 19, playing for the Warwickshire U21 side. Having represented Warwickshire,

the Midlands and the England Students side he played for England for the first time in 1997 on the tour to Argentina, scoring his first international try in the test in Buenos Aires. He joined Saracens later that summer, but switched to Bath for the 2001-02 season. Danny was educated at Woodlands School, Coventry.

International Record
1997 Arg (2), SA 1998 W (R), S (R), I (R), A, NZ (1), SA (R) 1999 S (R), A (R), USA, C World Cup It, NZ, Tg (R), SA 2000 SA (1, 2), A, Arg, SA 2001 W, It, S, I, A, Ro, SA, 2002 S (R), I (R), F (R), W, It, NZ, SA 2003 F (R), W (R), It, S (R), I (R),W, F (2), RWC U 2004 It, S, W, F NZ (1, 2R), C, SA, A 2005 W, F, I, It, S
Lions: 2001 A (1, 2, 3), 2005 NZ (1)

DID YOU KNOW?

Danny considers his finest rugby moments to be his first British Lions tour in 2001. Dave 'The Hawk' Thompson is his sporting hero for being "a great team player" who would do anything for his team. In 1996-97 he moved into the professional ranks with Coventry and still supports Coventry City FC. After his rugby career, Danny is interested in coaching.

ANDY HAZELL

FAST FACTS

CLUB	**Gloucester**
POSITION	**Flanker**
BORN	**25.4.78 Gloucester**
HEIGHT	**1.83m**
WEIGHT	**94kg**
CAPS	**6**
POINTS	**5 – 1t**

Andy Hazell won his first cap starting as open-side flanker in England's victory over Canada at Twickenham in November 2004 and another as replacement in the match against South Africa a week later. The Investec series represented his first serious breakthrough into the senior England team, but he made further inroads in the 2005 Six Nations. As well as starting in the opening match against Wales, Hazell appeared a further three times as a substitute, including a try-scoring appearance against Italy.

He took up the game aged 12 when he joined Old Richians, where he stayed for four years before joining another of his local teams, Gloucester Old Boys. His first representative game was for the South West U16s before joining the Premiership and making his debut at 19. He pulled on an England shirt for the first time playing for England U21s and was a member of the SANZAR squad that played in the Argentina competition back in 1999. In 2001 he played for the England XV that took on the Barbarians and also went on the England tour to North America, playing in both midweek games and scoring a try against British Columbia. His England A debut came in 2002 when he played against

Scotland at Headingley and he impressed throughout the 2003 England A Six Nations tournament. Andy was chosen for England's highly successful senior tour of New Zealand and Australia in June 2003 and played in the 23-9 victory over New Zealand Maori in New Plymouth, before flying to Vancouver to become a member of England's Churchill Cup-winning side in 2003, returning the following year. Injury meant he was unable to take part in the 2005 Churchill Cup. He was part of the wider 43 man England squad for the 2003 World Cup, but didn't make the final squad. He is a Gloucester player through and through and has flourished there as part of the Powergen Cup-winning side of 2003 and the side that finished top of the 2003 Zurich Premiership.

International Record
2004 C, SA (R) 2005 W, F (R), It (R), S (R)

DID YOU KNOW?

Andy was a goalkeeper for his Severn Vale school team and Hucclecote FC before he switched to rugby at the age of 12. He's a tough competitor in Gloucester colours. Andy once ran out of the tunnel at Kingsholm and tore his toe ligaments when he got tangled up with matting, costing him three months out of the game as he had his big toe reconstructed. It also cost him another set of kit, as every time he gets a bad injury he ditches every piece of kit he was wearing at the time. The player who's had the biggest influence on him is his former teammate Andy Deacon, now retired. Music is his passion. In fact, he ran a mobile disco in his teens and still has all the equipment and thousands of CDs. He confesses to being a quiet, home bird. He got married in July to girlfriend Dilwyn.

ANDREW HIGGINS

FAST FACTS

CLUB	**Bath**
POSITION	**Centre/Wing**
BORN	**13.07.81 Epping**
HEIGHT	**1.82m**
WEIGHT	**88kg**
CAPS	**Uncapped**

The injury to England and Bath World Champion centre Mike Tindall in December 2004 allowed Andrew Higgins to emerge as a real lynchpin for Bath. One of the most promising outside centres in the country, he showed his class in Bath's semi-final Premiership victory over Gloucester. A player gifted with great pace and an incredible strength that belies his 88kg frame, he has formed an effective club centre pairing with England international Olly Barkley. Selected for England A against France A in February 2004, he had to withdraw after suffering a broken jaw whilst playing for Bath just days before. A member of England's Intermediate National Academy squad for 2004-05, Andy has been highly-rated since his school days. Having joined Bath from Bristol Shoguns in the summer of 2003, he scored twice on his Zurich Premiership debut against Rotherham and went on to make 22 appearances during the 2003-04 season, scoring six tries. He learnt the game at the Christ's Hospital School, Sussex, and although injury cost him an England U16 Group Schools cap, he did go on to play for the England U18 Group. Andrew also earned an England U19 cap and, particularly impressively, he was a member of the England U21 squad for three seasons, playing in both the SANZAR and the U21 World Cups. Andy played for Worcester Warriors for two seasons before joining Bristol Shoguns in 2000-01. He was a member of the England Sevens squad in 2003-04 and this season was part of the wider squad available for the IRB Sevens series and the Rugby World Cup Sevens. He was called up late to the 2005 Churchill Cup.

DID YOU KNOW?

Andrew played outside centre to Australian double World Cup winner and captain Jason Little while at Bristol Shoguns. The 75 times-capped Little was a player he respected hugely and learnt a lot from during their time together. At school Andrew played a lot of football, mainly up front, and was also a county standard 100-metre sprinter. He also played in one of the most successful Christ's Hospital School rugby sides, unbeaten for almost four years. He says his best and worst rugby moment came at Twickenham at the same time, as a member of the Bath side that was beaten by London Wasps in the 2004 Zurich Championship final. Andy enjoys reading and travelling down to Devon and Cornwall to do some surfing.

CHARLIE HODGSON

FAST FACTS

CLUB	**Sale Sharks**
POSITION	**Fly half**
BORN	**12.11.80 Halifax**
HEIGHT	**1.77m**
WEIGHT	**82kg**
CAPS	**19**
POINTS	**154 – 4t, 31c, 22p, 2dg**

Charlie Hodgson made a welcome return to action during the 2003-04 season after having been sidelined from the game for eight months with a badly ruptured knee. He played at fly half for England during the 2004 summer tour to the southern hemisphere and was also the man in position for all three Investec Challenge internationals in 2004 when he was named 'Man of the Match' against Canada. Charlie's knee problems denied him selection for the 2003 World Cup and another injury kept him out of the side for the 2004 RBS 6 Nations. But he made a successful return in the white number 10 shirt, starting in all three test matches against New Zealand and Australia in the summer. Although he was an ever present during the Six Nations in 2005, Charlie struggled with his kicking in the opening matches of the tournament against Wales and France. By the end of the competition, however, Charlie had won over most of his critics with some strong all-round performances. Sir Clive Woodward was also impressed with Charlie's form for Sale Sharks during the remainder of the season, which ensured he made it onto the Lions tour to New Zealand. An intuitive footballer with a great eye for an opening and an extremely accurate place kicker, Charlie marked his England debut with a record-breaking 44-point haul against Romania back in November 2001, the most points scored by any England player in a test match, when England won 134-0. Educated at Bradford Grammar School, Charlie has also played for Old Brodleians, Durham University and Yorkshire. His time at Bradford Grammar School, under the watchful eye of well-known coach Geoff Wappett, really shaped his career. And although he was unfortunate to miss out on an England 16 Group cap when he managed to break his wrist in the final trial, Charlie did later go on to play for the 18 Group.

International Record

2001 Ro 2002 S (R), I (R), It (R), Arg 2003 F, W, It (R) 2004 NZ (1&2) A, C, SA, A
2005 W, F, I, It, S

DID YOU KNOW?

Charlie was a huge Halifax rugby league fan long before he ever tried his hand at the union code – and that switch came by chance. A friend of the family invited him along one Sunday morning to Old Brodleians rugby club and his first game was for the opposition, as they were a man short. It's not surprising Charlie rates his first full England cap against Romania and his 44 points scored in the game as one of his favourite rugby memories to date. His worst moment was picking up the anterior cruciate ligament injury against Italy in the 2003 RBS 6 Nations that kept him out for eight months. Tim Horan is the player he most respects.

STUART HOOPER

FAST FACTS

CLUB	**Leeds Tykes**
POSITION	**Lock**
BORN	**18.11.81 Exeter**
HEIGHT	**1.95m**
WEIGHT	**112kg**
CAPS	**Uncapped**

Stuart joined Leeds Tykes in June 2003 from Saracens, having represented England at U21 level. He broke into the Saracens team while still a teenager and played alongside French legend Abdel Benazzi in the second row. He made over 30 appearances for the Watford outfit before moving north. He was pressed into immediate action at Headingley when Tom Palmer was injured on tour in the summer of 2003. That started an impressive first season for 'Hoops' and gave Tykes fans a taste of his future potential. He made 20 starts in his first season and appeared in 17 out of 22 Zurich Premiership games. Originally from Devon, Hooper went to Ivybridge Community College, the school also attended by Tykes teammate Chris Bell. Stuart has all the attributes for a long and successful career. Despite a shaky start to 2004-05 because of injury, Stuart ended the season playing a major role in his club's Powergen Cup win over Bath and in their successful Premiership survival battle. He captained the side in three of their final winning matches against Leicester Tigers, NEC Harlequins and Bath.

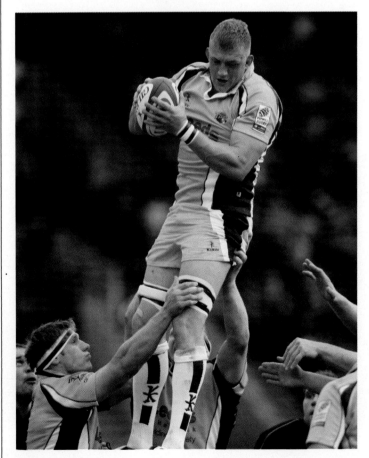

DID YOU KNOW?

Stuart could have been a league basketball star, having played the game at county level until he was 16, before opting for rugby on his move to the specialist sports campus at Ivybridge Community College in Devon. Like his current team mate Chris Bell, who attended Ivybridge a year behind him, Stuart rates coach Malcolm Collins as one of the biggest influences on his game before joining Saracens. Another huge influence was England flanker Richard Hill during his time at the north London club. He also admires England locks Danny Grewcock, Martin Johnson and Steve Borthwick. If Stuart had not become a professional player, there's little doubt that he would now be pursuing a career as a chef or restaurateur. His love of cooking, particularly Thai, comes from his mother, Gail, whom he describes as a 'fantastic cook'. Walking in the Lake District is another passion.

CHRIS JONES

FAST FACTS

CLUB	Sale Sharks
POSITION	Lock/Back row
BORN	24.8.80 Manchester
HEIGHT	1.98m
WEIGHT	95kg
CAPS	6
POINTS	5 – 1t

Chris Jones made giant strides in 2003 as a talented lock forward/flanker with pace and superb handling ability. This season his versatility proved an invaluable asset in times of injuries, strengthening England's back row against Wales following an injury to Lewis Moody. Indeed the Sale Shark is one of the most productive lineout men in the Zurich Premiership. A product of Stockport Grammar School and Sheffield Hallam University, he played for Cheshire at U18 and U20 level, then briefly with Fylde before joining Sale Sharks' senior side. He made a startling rise to the England Sevens squad and was nominated for the 2003 PRA Young Player of the Year Award. He was part of the England A team that beat France A, Scotland A and Italy A in their 2003 RBS 6 Nations and also went on the unbeaten England tour to North America and Japan that year. He also played for England in the uncapped match against the Barbarians at Twickenham in May 2003. His outstanding lineout jumping has made him a constant threat to other Zurich Premiership teams, while a series of long range tries for Sale Sharks has underlined his athletic capabilities. The year 2004 marked another leap forward. He was called up to the senior team by then Head Coach Clive Woodward from the start of the RBS 6 Nations. He came off the bench against Italy for his debut cap and promptly scored a try. This earned him a starting position against Scotland as flanker and again against Wales. He made the 2004 summer tour, starting against the All Blacks in Dunedin in the first test. Chris played in both of England's 2005 Churchill Cup matches.

International Record
2004 It (R), S, I (R), W, NZ (1) 2005 W

DID YOU KNOW?

Chris was stunned just before his first game for Sale Sharks when he had his boots cleaned by World Champion teammate Jason Robinson. It happened prior to a European Cup match when Jason wasn't registered to play. Another teammate, Brian Redpath, also commands Chris' great respect. An all rounder as a schoolboy enjoying cricket, his rugby career blossomed when he moved up into the senior school of Stockport Grammar and came under the influence of coach Chris Wright. Chris went on to take a Business Studies course at Sheffield Hallam University and was three years into it when Sale Sharks invited him to join them. Chris is also a movie fanatic and has built up a huge DVD collection.

BEN KAY MBE

FAST FACTS

CLUB	Leicester Tigers
POSITION	Lock
BORN	14.12.75 Liverpool
HEIGHT	1.98m
WEIGHT	119kg
CAPS	40
POINTS	10 – 2t

Benedict James Kay confirmed his status as a core member of the England squad in the World Cup when he started in all but one of England's games, including the unforgettable final in Sydney. More recently, he appeared twice as a replacement in the Investec Challenge series in 2004. Having joined Leicester Tigers from Waterloo in 1999, Ben was a member of the Tigers' Heineken European Cup winning sides in 2001 and 2002 as his international career blossomed. Having made his England A debut against France A in Blagnac in 2000, he led England A to a 23-22 win over France A at Redruth in April 2001 and was then called up for England's successful tour of North America that summer. Ben had previously represented England in the 1996 Students World Cup in South Africa and at U18, U19 and U21 level.

Ben has been in every starting line up for England in the 2002, 2003 and 2004 RBS 6 Nations, was part of the famous 2002 victory in Argentina and also played his part in historic wins against New Zealand and Australia on the pre-World Cup 2003 summer tour. He partnered then captain Martin Johnson in the national team's second row on many occasions and many consider him worthy of following Johnson as an England captain in the future. Although Ben was given a well-earned rest after the 2004 Six Nations and then benched for that year's autumn tests, he returned to the England starting line-up in 2005 and was an ever-present in partnership with Danny Grewcock in Andy Robinson's second row throughout the tournament. He was educated at Merchant Taylors, Crosby and Loughborough University and has also played rugby for Queensland University. British and Irish Lions Head Coach Sir Clive Woodward again showed how highly he rates Kay when he selected him for the 2005 tour to New Zealand.

International Record
2001 C (1, 2), A, Ro, SA (R) 2002 S, I, F, W, It, Arg, NZ (R), A, SA 2003 F (1+3), W, It, S, I, NZ, A, Rugby World Cup G, SA, Sam, W, F, A 2004 It, S, I, W, F, C (R), SA (R) 2005 W, F, I, It, S
Lions: 2005 NZ (1)

DID YOU KNOW?

Ben first started playing rugby for Waterloo minis and remembers Mike Slemen at Waterloo being extremely influential on his rugby development. His earliest sporting success came with the England U18s and that remains one of Ben's favourite memories from his early rugby career. Ben recognises Bath and England player Danny Grewcock as one of his toughest opponents and is always happy when he gets to play with him in England colours rather than against him. He admits to being a real gadgets man, always seen with a palm pilot or something technical in his hand. Ben has dipped his toe into TV rugby commentary and certainly enjoys it. But he really had a secret desire to appear on 'The A Team' TV series.

ALEX KING

FAST FACTS

CLUB	London Wasps
POSITION	Fly half
BORN	17.1.75 Brighton
HEIGHT	1.82m
WEIGHT	92kg
CAPS	5
POINTS	23 – 1t, 3p, 3c, 1dg

There are many, particularly those of the Wasps-loving persuasion, who believe Alexander David King should have more than five England caps. A talented fly half who knows how to get a backline moving, King again orchestrated things as London Wasps showed Leicester Tigers how to win the play-offs when they crushed Martin Johnson's outfit in the 2005 final. Alex was also a kingpin of the outstanding London Wasps team which won the Zurich Premiership and Heineken Cup double in the season 2003-04, a fitting signpost in the career of one of England rugby's finest game controllers.

The former Rosslyn Park player joined London Wasps in 1996 and helped them win the League that year, as well as kicking them to victory in the 2000 Tetley's Bitter Cup final. He scored a try on his England debut in 1997 and made his first test appearance at Twickenham as a replacement against South Africa in 1998. He earned his fifth cap against Wales in a World Cup warm-up match in Cardiff in August 2003. However, an injury acquired during the game ultimately affected his selection prospects for the World Cup and he stayed at home. It was Wasps' gain. In the Zurich Premiership he had enjoyed a glittering climax to 2003, being 'Man of the Match' in the Premiership final and amassing 24 points as London Wasps beat Gloucester 39-3. He finished as the leading Premiership points scorer, including play offs, with 284 points. In 2003-04 his performances continued at the same elevated standard. His tactical nous and educated left boot placed him at the helm of the Wasps double.

International Record
1997 Arg (R) 1998 SA (R) 2000 It (R) 2001 C (R) 2003 W

DID YOU KNOW?

Alex has a degree in economics and accountancy, which he started at Bristol University and finished off at Brunel University after turning professional. He has always been a fly half, so it's not surprising that Rob Andrew influenced him early on in his career. Aussie centre Tim Horan was another influence. He also enjoyed playing behind the London Wasps Dallaglio/Howley combination and is now enjoying his game alongside scrum half Matt Dawson. Away from rugby Alex likes to read thrillers or a biography and enjoys cooking. He also plays cricket and is a reasonable standard golfer, with a 15 handicap.

fan fare events
world rugby

ABTA
V064X

Emirates Airline Dubai Rugby7's

30 Nov – 2 Dec '05

Rugby in the sun!
Join Fan Fare Events in Dubai for the best in 7's rugby. Prices start from **£795**

Prices include return flights, 5 nights accommodation and tickets to all 3 days of competition.

HKG Rugby 7's

31 March – 02 April 2006

This year sees the 30th anniversary of the Hong Kong Rugby 7's. See this prestigious event with Fan Fare Events. Prices from **£749**

Prices include return flights, 4 nights hotel acommodation and tickets to all 3 days of competition.

RBS Six Nations

Italy v England
11 Feb 2006

France v England
12 March 2006

Prices from **£465**

England v Wales:	04 Feb
France v Ireland:	11 Feb
Scotland v England:	25 Feb
France v Italy:	25 Feb
Ireland v Wales:	26 Feb
Italy v Scotland:	18 March

Wales start the defence of their six nations crown against world champions England in what promises to be a very tight championship race.

Heineken European Cup

21-23 October 2005
Toulouse v Llanelli Scarlets

28-30 October 2005
Stade Francois v Leicester
Benetton Treviso v Saracens

9-11 December
Calvisano v Cardiff Blues

13-15 January 2006
Toulouse v London Wasps
Calvisano v Leeds Tykes

20-22 January 2006
Biarritz v Saracens

Prices start from **£199** per person. Price based on 2 nights, twin share accommodation at a 4 star hotel including breakfast and sideline match tickets.
Great value rugby weekends!

Autumn Internationals

See the cream of the southern hemisphere take on the best the six nations have to offer this autumn. Fan Fare Events can offer official RFU hospitality packages to all games*. (travel packages also available)

France v Australia:	5 Nov
Wales v N. Zealand:	5 Nov
England v Australia:	12 Nov
England v N.Zealand:	19 Nov
Wales v South Africa:	19 Nov
France v South Africa:	26 Nov

fan fare events
PRESENTS

usa ★
sports tours

tel: 0161 437 0002
www.usasportstours.com

Rugby World Cup, France

7 Sept. – 20 Oct. 2007

The Rugby World Cup moves to France in 2007 and Fan Fare Events will be offering full travel packages including match tickets for this great event.

Register now.
Contact Fan Fare Events to pre-register

For more information on these or any other sporting events simply call us on:

0161 437 0002
 or visit
www.fanfare-events.com

*Fan Fare Events are a sub-agent of an official RFU hospitality licensee

JOSH LEWSEY MBE

FAST FACTS

CLUB	**London Wasps**
POSITION	**Full back/Wing**
BORN	**30.11.76 Bromley**
HEIGHT	**1.80m**
WEIGHT	**86kg**
CAPS	**34**
POINTS	**105 – 21t**

Owen Joshua Lewsey must now surely be among the first names on the England team sheet. Able to play on the wing or at full back, he played in every 6 Nations match in 2005 and got on the scoresheet twice as he crossed the white line against Scotland and France. He was also a fixture for England in their three-match Investec Challenge programme in 2004, one of the few World Cup finalists who started in the autumn series. He had an impressive 2003 World Cup, including scoring five tries in the 111-13 drubbing of Uruguay. It equalled the record for the most tries scored in a test match, held jointly by Rory Underwood against Fiji in 1989 and Daniel Lambert against France in 1907. He put in a stunning Six Nations performance at Twickenham in 2002, seizing the chance handed to him by an injury to Jason Robinson, to score twice in the 40-5 win over Italy. He followed it up with the opening try in his next match against Scotland and was part of the Grand Slam winning side in Dublin in 2003. Josh earned his international call up after impressing for London Wasps and England A and was a key member of the England side that won the Hong Kong Sevens in 2002. Josh was first capped at the age of 21 on England's 'Tour from Hell' in Australia 1998 – the year he joined London Wasps from Bristol – and also appeared in all three tests in the summer 2001 tour to North America. He played a key part in both tests against New Zealand and Australia on the June 2003 southern hemisphere tour and few will forget his tackle on Aussie full back Mat Rogers towards the end of their 25-14 win over Australia in Melbourne. He has played a critical role for his club, too, reaching the finals of both the Heineken Cup and Zurich Premiership in 2004, winning the latter again in 2005. The versatile attacking three quarter grew up in Hertfordshire, where he attended Watford Boys Grammar School and played for the Amersham & Chiltern club. He had a full 2005 Lions experience starting in all three tests.

International Record

1998 NZ (1,2), SA (1) 2001 C (1, 2), USA 2003 It, S, I, NZ, A, F (2, 3R), RWC G, SA, U, F, A 2004 It, S, I, W, F, NZ (1&2) A, C, SA, A 2005 W, F, I, It, S Lions: 2005 NZ (1, 2, 3)

DID YOU KNOW?

Winning in Melbourne against Australia on the 2003 summer tour was a career highlight for Josh prior to his many World Cup experiences. He admires Sean Fitzpatrick for his mental toughness. In his spare time Josh likes to walk his boxer dogs Olaf and Wyn in the countryside near his 17th century home and also goes surfing. As the prospect of the World Cup approached in 2003, he had to choose between a full time career in the army and rugby. Josh could have played for Wales as his mother is Welsh and his father is half Welsh. One brother plays for London Welsh, another represented Wales U21s and all his uncles are in Welsh male choirs. But Josh is still very proud to be English.

More Tickets More Often

The England Rugby Supporters Club (ERSC) was launched by the RFU to help promote and support England Rugby and make the game more accessible to supporters like you.

We've achieved a great deal since we started in 2003 and are proud to say that we now offer our members a 1 in 4 change of obtaining a pair of tickets to watch England play in a grade A international fixture e.g. South Africa, Australia, France or Scotland.

Members Welcome Pack

In fact, during the last season (2004/5) we did actually offer every member the opportunity of purchasing tickets to watch England at a home international. Members were offered exclusive 3-day priority booking periods for both England v Canada and England v Italy before these matches went on public sale.

We also offer our members £5 discounts on tickets for games such as the annual Tibco Challenge England XV v Barbarians, Powergen Cup and Premiership Final. Using this benefit members have saved over £80,000 to date.

Following the redevelopment of Twickenham's South Stand the ERSC will receive a further allocation of tickets with the increase in stadium capacity.

Members will also have exclusive access to their own bar built inside the stadium.

It costs just £39 for 12 months membership, which entitles you to the following benefits:

- The right to enter the international ticket ballots to watch England play at Twickenham
- 10% discount in the Rugby Store
- Discounts on tickets for other major games at Twickenham
- Exclusive website with news and info direct from the England camp
- Free subscription to England Rugby Magazine – delivered to your door!
- Members only events and opportunities to meet players
- Fortnightly E-zine with exclusive competitions and prizes
- A great members welcome pack full of exclusive England Rugby merchandise.

Membership also makes a great gift and we have overseas and junior options available as well.

If you'd like to join or want more information –
Visit www.rfu.com/ersc
Call 0870 240 1642
Email englandsupporters@rfu.com

England Rugby would like to thank the following who generously support the game:

LEE MEARS

FAST FACTS

CLUB	Bath
POSITION	Hooker
BORN	05.03.79 Torquay
HEIGHT	1.75m
WEIGHT	102kg
CAPS	Uncapped

Tipped for future England success, Lee joined the Bath Academy from Colston's Collegiate School in 1997. And, while he managed to score on his first XV debut in a friendly against Saracens, it's only been in the past season that he's started to command a regular place in the starting line up. Hookers Andy Long, Mark Regan and more recently Jonathan Humphreys have all consigned him to the bench, but with Long and Regan moving on and Humphreys injured for much of the 2004-05 season, Lee seized the opportunity of a regular starting place to make a real impact. He has suffered criticisms that he is too small, but he is solidly built and his all round ability as a footballer cannot be ignored. He's a strong runner with the ball in hand, whilst also a powerful scrummager and his lineout play is exceptional. Lee started playing as a Torquay Athletic mini and, via Paignton College, eventually came under the current England Head Coach Andy Robinson and Alan Martinovich's guidance when at Colston's Collegiate. He has played for the England U16 and U18 Schools sides, the England U19s and England U21s, with whom he played in three World Cup matches in New Zealand. He was also a member of England's 2004 Churchill Cup squad, but it was in 2005 in the Churchill Cup tournament and against the Barbarians when he impressed.

DID YOU KNOW?

Lee loves to cook for himself and wife Danielle and has even done a couple of cookery courses to expand his talent and knowledge of food. Another passion is flying and although he hasn't got his pilot's license yet, he's flown gliders. In 1997 he was a member of the unbeaten England U18 Schools team that toured Australia and included the likes of Jonny Wilkinson, Mike Tindall, Iain Balshaw and Steve Borthwick. Being part of Bath's starting line-up for the 2005 Powergen Cup final has been his career highlight to date. His ambition is simply to be as good as he possibly can be. He also enjoys golf, with a handicap of 18.

UGO MONYE

FAST FACTS

CLUB	NEC Harlequins
POSITION	Wing
BORN	13.04.83 London
HEIGHT	1.85m
WEIGHT	84kg
CAPS	Uncapped

Ugo Monye has all the qualities needed to perform at the very top of his profession. His blistering pace, mixed with his raw power and aggression, can shatter any defence he's up against. He made his Premiership debut in November 2002 and ended the season scoring two tries against London Wasps in May 2003 and another just eight days later in their Zurich Wild Card semi-final against Leicester Tigers. He started the 2003-04 season in similar vein, touching down five tries in his opening two games, including a hat trick against Rotherham. In 2003 he also burst onto the IRB World Sevens Series stage with the England Sevens squad. His speed off the mark helped him score twice in the Brisbane final as England swept to the first of their three sevens titles that season. He also played an important part in their other tournament wins in Hong Kong and in the final round at Twickenham. He's another top class player to have come out of Jonny Wilkinson's old Hampshire school, Lord Wandsworth College, and played for Hampshire U17s and U20s. Ugo was also an outstanding track athlete who appeared in the English Schools Athletics Association Championships at U17 and U20 age groups. He has represented England at U19 and U21 level and played in both the 2003 and 2004 U21 World Cups. Ugo was nominated for try of the season in the 2004-05 Zurich Premiership for his effort against Leicester Tigers.

DID YOU KNOW?

Ugo had achieved the Olympic 100 metres qualifying time of 10.6 seconds by the time he was 16. Having reached the National Championships twice and won an U20 bronze medal in the 4 x 100m event it was always a tough call as to which sport he would ultimately concentrate on. His sports master Tim Richardson, however, put him in touch with NEC Harlequins U19 coach Colin Osborne and when the club offered him a professional contract after a few games, he jumped at the opportunity. Within 12 months he was a member of the England Sevens team that won the Hong Kong Sevens. His club captain Andre Vos is a player he admires immensely along with another former club mate Jason Leonard and the Underwood brothers Rory and Tony. Apart from playing for England, he also has a burning ambition to play in the same side as his 19-year-old brother. A man with strong Christian values and beliefs, Ugo's other passions include reading and music. He loves R&B and hip hop.

LEWIS MOODY MBE

FAST FACTS

CLUB	Leicester Tigers
POSITION	Flanker
BORN	3.6.78 Ascot
HEIGHT	1.93m
WEIGHT	102kg
CAPS	31
POINTS	40 – 8t

Lewis Walton Moody won his 24th England cap when he came on as a replacement in the 2003 Rugby World Cup final to help England beat Australia. He played a part in all seven World Cup matches, demonstrating the tenacious and eye-catching performances that hallmark his career. He won the fateful final lineout in the phase of play that led to Jonny Wilkinson's epoch-making drop goal. Moody, the 2001 Zurich England Young Player of the Season, won his first three caps playing in all three North American tour tests in June 2001, scoring against the US Eagles in San Francisco. He was then called up to the senior squad for the match against Ireland in Dublin in October 2001 and came on to win cap number four. He has now scored eight tries for England, including one against the Wallabies in last November's Investec Challenge series, another against the All Blacks in November 2002, and two in England's world record 134-0 win over Romania in November 2001. He became the youngest Leicester Tigers player to figure in a league game. He scored two tries for England Colts against Wales in April 1997, and was also a member of the side that won the Madrid Sevens at the end of that same season. He also played in both of the Tigers' European Cup wins in 2001 and 2002 and was a member of the Tigers' Premiership squad during their winning run in the four seasons between 1998-2002. An ankle injury picked up in December 2003 ruled him out of the rest of that season but he battled back brilliantly, returning for his club in October 2004 in the Heineken European Cup match against Calvisano, and for England one month later, when he started in all three of the Investec Challenge matches at Twickenham. He further proved that he was back to his best during the following Six Nations where he played in four of England's five matches, missing only the opening defeat to Wales. Sir Clive Woodward also showed faith in Moody by taking him on the 2005 British Lions tour to New Zealand where he played a central role.

International Record

2001 C (1, 2),USA, I (R), Ro, SA (R) 2002 I (R), W, It, Arg, NZ, A, SA 2003 F(1, 2, 3), W, Rugby World Cup G (R), SA, Sm (R), Ur, W, F (R), A (R), C, SA, A 2005 F, I, It, S Lions: 2005 NZ (2,3)

DID YOU KNOW?

Coming off the bench to play in the final of the Rugby World Cup understandably counts as Lewis' finest moment in his rugby career. He judges Jonah Lomu as one of his toughest opponents. When he was five he took up mini rugby at Bracknell, when a school friend suggested he join him, and Alan Gunner of Bracknell is one of many coaches Lewis remembers helping him in his career. If Lewis had not become a professional rugby player he would have chosen to join the army, or to study architectural design. His golf handicap is 28 and he enjoys wakeboarding as well as waterskiing.

ROBBIE MORRIS

FAST FACTS

CLUB	Newcastle Falcons
POSITION	Prop
BORN	20.02.82 Hertford
HEIGHT	1.88m
WEIGHT	121kg
CAPS	2
POINTS	0

Robbie Morris is a very versatile front row player and happily plays on either side of the scrum. He won his first England cap against Wales in 2003, two days after celebrating his 21st birthday, and his second against Italy a fortnight later. He had previously toured Argentina with England in the summer of 2002, scoring a try against the Pumas A team. He is a product of the Northampton Academy system, having joined Saints from Hertford RFC in 2000. It followed a distinguished junior career when he played for Hertfordshire at every age group and went on to feature in the London Division 18 Group Clubs team and the England 18 Group Clubs side before signing professional forms. He was picked for the England XV against the Barbarians in May 2004, but unfortunately suffered a leg injury that prevented him taking his place on the 2004 Churchill Cup tour shortly afterwards. He was also on the bench for the England A team that defeated France A 30-20 at Bath in February, the only A international of the 2004-05 season. Next season he is moving to Newcastle Falcons.

International Record:
2003 W, It

DID YOU KNOW?

Robbie was an exceptional field athlete as a youngster and won a silver medal in the discus as a member of the England athletics team that competed at the Youth Commonwealth Games in Edinburgh in 2000. He was also selected for the Great Britain team at junior level in the shot put, but eventually decided to concentrate on rugby as it offered him a full time career. Former Saints coach Wayne Smith was a big help to him when he was first at Franklin's Gardens, where he made over 90 first team appearances. His two England caps are his prize possessions to date, although he hopes to add more before his playing days are through. When he's not playing, Robbie loves eating out or walking his two dogs, Bodie and Doyle.

JAMIE NOON

FAST FACTS

CLUB	Newcastle Falcons
POSITION	Centre
BORN	9.5.79 Goole
HEIGHT	1.80m
WEIGHT	86kg
CAPS	10
POINTS	20 – 4t

Jamie Noon capped an incredible season with a hat-trick of tries against Scotland in the 2005 RBS 6 Nations. He grew in confidence with every game after his slightly shaky start alongside club-mate Mathew Tait in Wales. But whereas Tait wasn't selected again, Noon ended up playing in every game of England's Six Nations campaign. It's impressive that he got there too, because after he had won three caps on England's North American tour in 2001 Noon had to wait two years before he once again pulled on an England shirt. He played in England's 43-9 World Cup warm-up victory over Wales at the Millennium Stadium, Cardiff, in August 2003. Earlier in the year he had impressed when coming on as a replacement for England A against France – immediately creating a try for Joe Worsley. A natural defender whose good vision creates opportunities for others, he was considered unlucky to miss out to Mike Catt in England's World Cup squad and not to play in the 2004 Investec Challenge series. Jamie has been a major asset in the Newcastle Falcons' Zurich Premiership ranks and is widely regarded as one of the most incisive runners in the game. He played an important part in the Falcons' fight for league survival in 2002-03 and was also a key member of their Powergen Cup-winning side in April 2004. His early career started at Fyling Hall School, playing in the back row. At Whitby he switched to fly half, scrum half and wing. With the aid of a Falcons scholarship, he attended Northumbria University and toured Argentina and New Zealand with England U21s. He has also represented English Universities, England Sevens and England A in 2002-03 and was the star player of the back division during England's 2004 Churchill Cup summer tour to Canada.

International Record
2001 C (1, 2), USA 2003 W, F (2, R) 2005 W, F, I, It, S

DID YOU KNOW?

Jamie thought he would make a good flanker before Newcastle Falcons Kiwi Academy coach Paul McKinnon turned him into a centre. "Without his insight I don't think I would be where I am today," he admits. Some career highlights include being a member of England's first ever winning Hong Kong Sevens side and playing at Twickenham in his club's 2001 Powergen Cup win over NEC Harlequins. Martin Johnson and Jonny Wilkinson, his club mate and guitar partner, are among the players he most admires. Jamie graduated in 2002 with a degree in Sports & Exercise Science and in July 2004 he married Rachel. He likes squash, golf, gardening and sea fishing – and loves animals. After rugby Jamie would like to study zoology.

TOM PALMER

FAST FACTS

CLUB	Leeds Tykes
POSITION	Lock
BORN	27/03/79 London
HEIGHT	1.98m
WEIGHT	110kg
CAPS	1
POINTS	0

The Leeds Tyke started as a five-year-old mini with the Barnet club, but was very soon winging his way north to Scotland with his family where he played for Boroughmuir School until he was 16 and then for the Boroughmuir club itself. With his family on the move again he spent 18 months at the Otago Boys High School where he played for New Zealand Schoolboys, before returning to this country to start a degree course in physics at Leeds University. It was there that Tom was picked up by the Leeds Tykes club and his Scottish connections also earned him selection for the Scotland U19 and U21 sides. Having opted to play for England, he toured Canada and America with England in 2001 and has been a regular squad member ever since. He won his first senior cap as a replacement in the final 10 minutes of England's victory over the US Eagles in San Francisco in June of 2001. In the summer of 2003 he was selected for England's summer tour to New Zealand and then joined up with the Churchill Cup squad in Canada, only to pick up a serious knee injury that took six months to put right. In March 2004 he was made vice captain to Mike Catt in the England A side which was narrowly defeated 22-26 by France A.

International Record
2001 USA (R)

DID YOU KNOW?

Not surprisingly, fellow lock Martin Johnson is Tom's favourite player, plus France's former full back Serge Blanco for his attacking flair. Tom's mentor and Leeds Tykes coach Phil Davies is the man who's had the biggest influence on Tom's game; he's been under his wing since joining the club in 1997. Spotted by Davies in his first game for Leeds University, Tom played for Leeds Tykes U19s during his first year at college. He then studied part-time when he was drafted into the first team squad in September 1998. He finished his physics degree over the next three years, juggling his studies with the demands of professional rugby. Tykes' promotion at the end of 2000-2001 also ranks as one of his all-time favourite rugby moments, along with being on the New Zealand leg of the 2003 summer tour. Tom loves skiing, walking, biking and going to the cinema.

HENRY PAUL

FAST FACTS

CLUB	Gloucester
POSITION	Fly half/Centre
BORN	10.02.74 New Zealand
HEIGHT	1.80m
WEIGHT	93kg
CAPS	6
POINTS	6 – 3c

Henry Paul started all three of England's Investec Challenge matches in 2004. He is an imaginative distributor and all-round talent who has earned respect throughout rugby union after succeeding in switching codes. When still in league, he helped Bradford Bulls RL club beat Wigan Warriors in the Super League Grand Final in the autumn of 2001. Born in New Zealand, he and his brother Robbie qualify for England through their Liverpudlian grandfather. A prolific goal kicker and a gifted runner and distributor, Henry won national squad selection after just one game for Gloucester, having begun a four year contract at Kingsholm in 2001. He won a full England cap as a replacement against France in 2002 and has regularly excelled for the England Sevens side. He was a member of the England team that won the 2003 Churchill Cup in Canada and returned there on the 2004 Churchill Cup tour. Henry's distinguished career in rugby league included 23 caps for New Zealand. He was tempted away from the Bradford Bulls to play union for Gloucester by Tom Walkinshaw and Philippe Saint Andre and had a dream debut, scoring 28 points against Caerphilly. Ten games later he had reached the century mark. Henry returned to the England squad for the 2004 RBS 6 Nations, coming off the bench in Rome and Murrayfield and was considered 'Man of the Match' for England A against France A in March with five penalties and a conversion and all round play of high class. He has now settled as inside centre for Gloucester after earlier periods at full back and fly half. His long passing is a trademark of Gloucester's style.

International Record
2002 F (R) 2004 It (R), S (R) C, SA, A

DID YOU KNOW?

As a 17-year-old Henry played softball for the New Zealand U19 team in the Auckland World Series games alongside Jeremy Stanley, son of All Black legend Joe. A year later he had moved to Wigan. His early career started at the tender age of three with the Ponsonby club and later, during his time at Rutherford High, he played union during the week and league at the weekends. His personal highlights include selection for both the New Zealand rugby league team and England's rugby union side. Wigan's 1995 Rugby League Challenge Cup Final appearance at Wembley is also high on his list. To relax he is learning guitar. He loves playing with his seven-year-old son Theo and his baby daughter Milan. Henry is currently teaching Theo to play golf and football. Henry's own golfing handicap is a cool 14.

PETER RICHARDS

FAST FACTS

CLUB	**Gloucester**
POSITION	**Scrum half/Fly half/Centre**
BORN	**10.03.78**
HEIGHT	**1.80m**
WEIGHT	**89kg**
CAPS	**Uncapped**

Peter is a player who can make things happen out of nothing and turn a game in an instant with a piece of his own personal creativity. He's also a very versatile player as he's demonstrated at London Wasps where he has played in any one of three positions; scrum half – his preferred role – fly half and centre. His rugby career began with Jonny Wilkinson playing mini rugby at Farnham Rugby Club, before they both went to Lord Wandsworth College, Hampshire, and worked their way through the age groups as the school's half back combination. He featured in both the England U16 and U18 Group Schools teams before joining London Irish in 1996. He quickly made his first team debut against Leicester Tigers and represented England at U19, U21 and A level before joining NEC Harlequins for the 1999-2000 season. He left two years later and spent a year in Italy playing for Benetton Treviso, then returned to join Bristol Shoguns. He moved again, to London Wasps at the start of the 2003-04 season when Shoguns were relegated from the Zurich Premiership. Pete moves to Gloucester next season to replace Andy Gomarsall. He was part of the England 'Tour of Hell' to Australia and New Zealand in 1998 when he played against the New Zealand Maori. He came home before the final leg to South Africa. He had a successful Churchill Cup tour in 2005.

DID YOU KNOW?

Pete played for Havant U8 team as a four year old before moving to Farnham and linking up with the Wilkinson brothers Mark and Jonny. He rates his dad Geoff, a good player for Eastern Counties and the London Division on the wing, as the biggest influence on his career, particularly while ferrying him to the England Schools matches and trials at Wolverhampton. He's not a bad footballer either and at 13 played for Southampton Schoolboys in central midfield. Nowadays he rates his former London Wasps team mate Rob Howley as the player he most respects, while his favourite rugby moment occurred in 2004 when he was part of the winning England Sevens team out in Hong Kong.

SIX DISC DVD
COLLECTORS BOX SET

RUGBY
WORLD CUP
2003

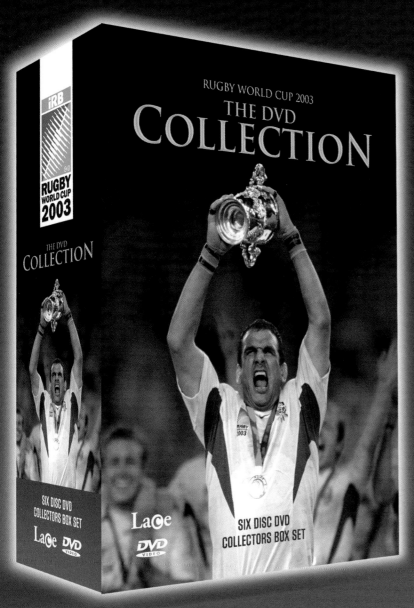

RUGBY WORLD CUP 2003
THE DVD
COLLECTION

SIX DISC DVD
COLLECTORS BOX SET

COMPRISES OF:

- THE OFFICIAL REVIEW
- GREATEST MOMENTS
- ENGLAND'S STORY
  (DOUBLE DVD)
- THE FINAL
  (DOUBLE DVD)

JASON ROBINSON MBE

FAST FACTS

CLUB	**Sale Sharks**
POSITION	**Full back/Centre/Wing**
BORN	**30.7.74 Leeds**
HEIGHT	**1.73m**
WEIGHT	**84kg**
CAPS	**39**
POINTS	**110 – 22t**

Jason Robinson continued in 2005 the way he left off in 2004, as England captain. For the first time in his union career Jason was honoured with the England captaincy for the three Investec Challenge matches in the autumn of 2004 and discharged his responsibilities with distinction on and off the pitch. So much so that he was then asked to continue in the role for the RBS 6 Nations and he led England out against Wales, France and Ireland before an injury put an end to his campaign. Not surprisingly, England's 'Billy Whiz' played in all seven of England's World Cup games in 2003 and scored the memorable try in the final, sending millions of England supporters into meltdown just before half time. He has run rings around opposing rugby union defences since his switch from rugby league in November 2000. Jason made his debut for Sale Sharks against Coventry after a glittering rugby league career for Wigan, in which he won 12 caps for Great Britain and seven for England. In all he played in 302 rugby league games, scoring 184 tries before switching codes. He won his first England cap as a substitute against Italy in February 2001, having played in the A match against Wales at Wrexham a fortnight earlier. He was immediately chosen for the 2001 Lions tour to Australia and was one of the outstanding players in the side that won the first test in Brisbane by 29-13, scoring a superb try, bursting past Chris Latham down the left wing. Not content with that, he scored another in the final test. Jason's speed off the mark and explosive side step make him one of the most popular, exciting and dangerous broken field runners in the world game, whether starting at full back or wing. In the 2004 RBS 6 Nations he scored three tries from the centre position in the opening match against Italy and was named 'Man of the Match'. Jason chose to opt out of the 2004 summer tour to recharge his batteries, having played constantly before, during and after the 2003 World Cup. He is currently captain of Sale Sharks.

International Record

2001 It (R) ,S (R), F (R), I, A, Ro, SA 2002 S, I, F, It, NZ, A, SA 2003 F (1&3), W, S, I, NZ, A, RWC G, SA, Sam, U (R), W, F, A 2004 It, S, I, W, F, C, SA, A 2005 W, F, I
Lions: 2001 A (1, 2, 3), 2005 NZ (1, 2)

DID YOU KNOW?

Jason was one of the first players to swap league for union when he played part of a season for Bath in 1996. Some of his heroes are from rugby league, including Gary Schofield and Ellery Hanley, whom he watched when he was young. He is particularly proud of the moment when he became a dual international. He lists another player who has excelled in both codes, Australian Wendell Sailor, as one of his toughest opponents. He is a devout Christian and family man, was educated at Matthew Murray High School, Leeds and chooses to teach his three children at home.

GRAHAM ROWNTREE

FAST FACTS

CLUB	**Leicester Tigers**
POSITION	**Prop**
BORN	**18.4.71 Stockton-on-Tees**
HEIGHT	**1.82m**
WEIGHT	**109kg**
CAPS	**52**
POINTS	**0**

Graham Christopher Rowntree is one of the great warriors of the Zurich Premiership, a Leicester Tigers stalwart and a rugged scrummager with fine all-round ability. His performances in England's three Investec Challenge autumn tests in 2004 were outstanding and revitalised his test career. Graham further proved himself by playing in four of England's 2005 Six Nations matches and earning himself a much-deserved call-up to Clive Woodward's Lions squad for the tour to New Zealand. Graham was educated at Hastings High School and John Cleveland College in Hinckley and has been with Leicester Tigers for 16 years since joining them from Nuneaton. For much of that time he was in harness with the famous 'ABC Club' alongside Richard Cockerill and Darren Garforth. He won his first England cap as a temporary replacement for Jason Leonard in the match against Scotland in 1995, a Grand Slam year. Graham appeared for both the England U16 and U18 Group Schools sides and in 1993 was the youngest player in Leicester's Cup-winning side at Twickenham. He also made the 1997 Lions tour of South Africa. He narrowly missed selection for England's squad of 30 for the 2003 World Cup and Clive Woodward admitted that the decision to leave Rowntree behind was one of the hardest he had to make in all his years as England Head Coach. Rowntree had played in both the 1995 and 1999 World Cups. He was prominent throughout the pre-World Cup victory years, starting in all of England's Six Nations games in 2002. He also played in England's magnificent 15-13 win over New Zealand in Wellington in 2003, as well as in the World Cup warm-up against France down in Marseille. This quietly-spoken and modest man has earned his reputation by simply getting on with his work, never trying to put the spotlight on his own efforts and always giving his all for the team.

International Record
1995 S (R), World Cup It, WS. WS, 1996 F, W, S, I, It, Arg, 1997 S, I, F, W, A 1998 A, NZ (1, 2), SA, N (R), It (R), 1999 USA, C, World Cup It (R), Tg, Fj (R), 2001 C (1, 2)USA, I(R), A, Ro, SA 2002 S, I, F ,W, It 2003 F (R), W, It, S, I, NZ, F (2) 2004 C, SA, A 2005 W, F, I, It
Lions: 1997, 2005 NZ (2R,3R)

DID YOU KNOW?

Graham is a strong family man. For eight years of his life until the game turned professional he worked as an insurance broker. He regards his Tigers teammates as the biggest influence on his career, although he singles out Martin Johnson for special praise, having played with him since their Tigers youth team days. For Graham, winning the European Cup in 2001 against Stade Francais will always be one of his favourite memories, along with the 15-13 defeat of New Zealand in Wellington in 2003. Now he wants to stay fit, stay healthy and play at the top for as long as he can.

PAUL SACKEY

FAST FACTS

CLUB	**London Wasps**
POSITION	**Wing**
BORN	**08.11.79 London**
HEIGHT	**1.82m**
WEIGHT	**90kg**
CAPS	**Uncapped**

Paul Sackey only took up the game at 16 when he went to the rugby-only John Fisher School in Purley and started out as a centre or full back. His pace earned him an immediate call up to the school's 1st XV and he was a member of their sevens team that won the Rosslyn Park Nationals Sevens Tournament two years running. He was quickly snapped up by a London Wasps scout and played for Wasps U19s and U21s before moving to Bedford. During his time there he was called up to the England U21 squad that played in the U21 World Cup in New Zealand before signing professional forms for London Irish and joining them in August 2000. That year Paul also played for the England Sevens team in Argentina, while in 2002 he was included in the England tour party that played the USA and Canada. He scored twice in the 83-21 win over the USA in Los Angeles. In 2003 he also played for England A against Ireland A.

A strong, willowy and elusive player, he topped the London Irish try-scoring list in 2000-01 and in four years scored 121 Premiership tries. Paul was a member of England's 2004 Churchill Cup squad that played Canada and the New Zealand Maori. He left London Irish in February 2005 to return to London Wasps and was immediately drafted into the first team squad, including playing at wing in their victorious Zurich Premiership final against Leicester Tigers. He impressed against the Barbarians and at the Churchill Cup in 2005.

DID YOU KNOW?

Paul's career has been guided throughout by England scrum half Andy Gomarsall. Gomarsall had taken Paul on a sevens trip to Lisbon and realised his potential, then brokered his move to Bedford and put him in touch with top fitness coach Margot Wells before his transfer to London Irish. Playing for Irish when they beat Northampton Saints 38-7 in the 2002 Powergen Cup final still remains the highlight of his career to date. Up to the time he went to the John Fisher School he had been a very good footballer, playing in central midfield for Coulsdon Athletic and also having trials for Crystal Palace. He's an excellent athlete, too, and as a young teenager was second in the 60 metre hurdles at the National Championships, also competing in the long jump and triple jump. To relax he likes dinner with his girlfriend, a movie, or listening to hip hop or R&B music. But his real passion is his car, a Mercedes AMG55.

PAT SANDERSON

FAST FACTS

CLUB	**Worcester Warriors**
POSITION	**Flanker**
BORN	**06.09.77 Chester**
HEIGHT	**1.90m**
WEIGHT	**93kg**
CAPS	**6**
POINTS	**5 – 1t**

Pat Sanderson is an intelligent, skilful and hard-working back row player who has ended a highly successful season as captain of Worcester Warriors by captaining the recent England XV against the Barbarians and England's Churchill Cup squad. He would have undoubtedly earned far more international caps but for injuries. Pat was first capped on England's 1998 southern hemisphere tour, facing New Zealand twice and South Africa, and he won another three caps on the 2001 tour to North America. He has also been a prolific England Sevens player, having made his debut back in 1997 in Hong Kong. In 2003-04 he played in six of the IRB World Series rounds, including the three wins in South Africa, Hong Kong and London. In 2002 he was also a member of England's Commonwealth Games squad in Manchester. His early 15-a-side career blossomed at Kirkham Grammar School where he won his first international cap for the England 16 Group Schools team. He joined Manchester Sale (now Sale Sharks) in 1996 and was capped by England U21s and England A. He moved to NEC Harlequins, where he played in the 2001 Powergen Cup final when Quins lost to Newcastle Falcons by 30-27. At the end of the 2003-04 season he moved to newly-promoted Worcester Warriors where, as captain, he was key in ensuring they stayed in the Premiership. Pat was nominated for the PRA Players' Player of the Year in 2004-05 and led England to Churchill Cup victory as captain in 2005.

International Record
1998 NZ (1, 2), SA 2001 C (1R, 2R), USA

DID YOU KNOW?

Pat is the elder brother of Alex, who played alongside him at Sale Sharks before their career paths diverged and Alex joined Saracens. Pat is the Chairman of the Professional Rugby Players' Association and he is well placed to understand the problems players face, particularly with injuries. A fractured shoulder, two damaged knees and a prolapsed disc have all kept him out of the game at different stages. He admits to being superstitious and hates to see a solitary magpie on the morning of a game. His first cap against New Zealand is one of his treasured memories, along with his appearance in the England Sevens side at the 2002 Commonwealth Games. He admires his brother Alex and Andre Vos, the Harlequins captain, as players. Away from the sport, Pat is involved in his property business.

SIMON SHAW MBE

FAST FACTS

CLUB	**London Wasps**
POSITION	**Lock**
BORN	**1.1.73 Nairobi, Kenya**
HEIGHT	**2.05m**
WEIGHT	**120kg**
CAPS	**28**
POINTS	**10 – 2t**

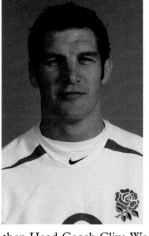

Simon Dalton Shaw is one of the most powerful forwards in rugby and so few were surprised when Clive Woodward called him up to the Lions squad this year after Malcolm O'Kelly's injury ruled him out of the tour. When he arrived in New Zealand, Simon will certainly have cast a thought back to a previous visit. His unexpected red card ten minutes into England's second Test against the All Blacks in Auckland 2004 led to a 14-man England fighting a heroic rearguard action – unfortunately in vain. Shaw won his first cap against Italy in 1996 and is one of the tallest men ever to play international rugby for England. He was a Bristol player before moving to London Wasps in 1997 and helping them lift the 1999 Tetley's Bitter Cup. In his younger days he had represented England Schools, Colts, Students and U21s after his education at Kings and Runnymede Colleges, Godalming Sixth Form College and the University of West of England, Bristol. His England career took off again in 2000 when he stood in for the injured Martin Johnson in the Six Nations and he appeared as a replacement in the 27-20 triumph over South Africa at Bloemfontein later the same year. He played in all three tests on the England tour of North America in 2001, scoring two tries in the 59-20 win over Canada at Burnaby. Simon played a part in all three World Cup warm-up games – against Wales (where he was voted 'Man of the Match') and as a replacement against France both in Marseille and at Twickenham. When England's 30-man squad was named for the World Cup, England's then Head Coach Clive Woodward described Shaw's omission as one of the hardest decisions he'd made in his time with England. However, Shaw became England's 31st player, sent out during the World Cup to replace the injured Danny Grewcock, though he did not get on to the field. He was immense throughout London Wasps' 2003-04 season where the club won the double, the Zurich Championship and Heineken Cup. He was voted Zurich Player of the Year. Shaw also toured South Africa with the 1997 Lions and is a Barbarian. And he was again a key figure in Wasps' stunning 2005 play off final win over Leicester Tigers.

International Record

1996 It, Arg, 1997 S, I, F, W, A, SA (R), 2000 I, F, ht W, Itnks, S, SA (1R, 2R), 2001 C (1R, 2), USA, I 2003 It (R), W (2), F (2R, 3R) 2004 It (R), S (R), NZ (1, 2) A
Lions: 1997

DID YOU KNOW?

Simon lived in Kenya until the age of 16. His father suggested he take up rugby, so he found himself thrown in at the deep end at 16, learning fast. He moved from schools to winning a divisional Colts championship. He played in Otago, New Zealand for a year before returning to play for Bristol in 1993 where he stayed for four years. If Simon had not become a professional rugby player he believes he would have run his own restaurant. He considers fellow England player Jason Robinson his toughest opponent because of his fast footwork.

be strong

SERIOUS EQUIPMENT FOR PEOPLE SERIOUS ABOUT STRENGTH TRAINING

powered by

You've got the drive to look great.

Only Nautilus has the optimal strength curve technology™ to help you get the results you want.

Success depends on getting results.

Nautilus is designed to a higher standard.

"At the Tigers, we require biomechanically sound, reliable, heavy duty equipment with an excellent after-sales service - Nautilus gives us this"
Phil Mack - Director of Athletic Performance & Medical Services, Leicester Tigers

www.nautilus.com

Nautilus, 4 Vincent Avenue - Crownhill, Milton Keynes MK8 0AB   Phone: +44 (0) 1908 267345   Fax: +44 (0) 1908 267 346   enquiries@nautilus.com

ANDREW SHERIDAN

PLAYER PROFILE

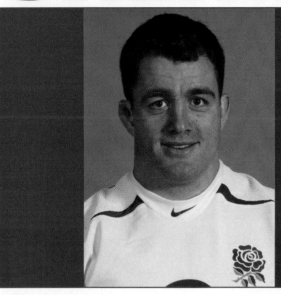

FAST FACTS

CLUB	**Sale Sharks**
POSITION	**Prop**
BORN	**01.11.79 Petts Wood**
HEIGHT	**1.95m**
WEIGHT	**119kg**
CAPS	**1**
POINTS	**0**

It's testament to the esteem in which Andrew Sheridan is held in some quarters that, even with just the one cap under his belt and not featuring at all for England during the 2005 RBS 6 Nations championship, Sir Clive Woodward deemed him worthy of a place among the 2005 Lions squad. Andrew has a reputation of being one of the strongest forwards in the game and can bench press twice his own weight and dead lift almost three times his own weight. Despite many people calling for Andrew to make his full international debut, the Sale Sharks prop had to bide his time and wait for his chance. The wait was finally over, though, when he took to the field to win his first cap as a replacement against Canada in November 2004. He first started playing rugby at the age of nine with Old Elthamians and was with them for five years until he went on to Dulwich College. There Andrew worked his way through the Surrey age group teams and was also capped by both the England U16 and U18 Group Schools teams as a second row forward. His first experience of professional rugby came when he joined Richmond in the 1998-99 season when they were playing at Reading's Madejski Stadium. Unfortunately, things were not going well at the club, but as the Zurich Premiership side folded, Andrew won a place in the England U21 squad that played in the 1999 SANZAR tournament in Argentina. On his return home he then joined Bristol. Andrew made around 80 appearances for the West Country outfit and converted from the second row to play loose-head prop. In 2000 he also went on England's tour to South Africa and in 2001-02 played for England A against Ireland A and France A. In 2003 he was in England's Churchill Cup squad in Canada, the USA and Japan and came back to join his new club, Sale Sharks, after Bristol's relegation from the Premiership. In December 2003 he also played for the England XV that took on the Barbarians immediately following England's

Rugby World Cup success. Many people expect to see Andrew continuing his progress in future in England colours.

International Record
2004 C (R)

DID YOU KNOW?

Andrew, also known as Sherri or Big Ted, is very serious about bricklaying and is currently in the second year of an NVQ qualification. He has also done a short plumbing course and without doubt would have been a builder had he not taken up a career as a professional rugby player. He has very diverse talents, including playing the guitar and writing his own country/folk-style songs. At school he was a good shot putter and came fifth in the England Schools Championship. The biggest influence on his career has been his family. Going on tour in 2000 with England to South Africa has been one of his career highlights along with gaining his first cap at Twickenham last November. Losing to Newcastle Falcons in the 2004 Powergen Cup final with Sale Sharks was, however, definitely a low point. Trevor Leota and Scott Quinnell are two players he admires.

JAMES SIMPSON-DANIEL

FAST FACTS

CLUB	Gloucester
POSITION	Wing
BORN	30.5.82 Stockton-on-Tees
HEIGHT	1.80m
WEIGHT	88kg
CAPS	7
POINTS	5 – 1t

James Simpson-Daniel is a talented back from a family of talented backs. Unluckily, injury once again prevented him playing a part in the 2004 Investec Challenge series in November and he missed further game time for the build up to this year's RBS 6 Nations.

His recent form demonstrated good pace in attack and hitting onto the ball hard, confirming he is capable of playing international rugby and making a difference. He narrowly missed selection to the final 30 for the 2003 World Cup, although he had celebrated his first RBS 6 Nations championship start some months earlier with a try in the match against Italy. In the autumn of 2002 he won two successive caps before missing the South Africa game through glandular fever. He had burst onto the Gloucester and England scene late in 2002 against New Zealand and made a magnificent try-scoring debut – in direct opposition to Jonah Lomu – in a non-capped England XV against the Barbarians at Twickenham in May of that year. His famous try, when he raced past Lomu on the outside, rapidly brought him to wider attention. He had toured Chile with the England U19s and shared in England's sevens success in Hong Kong. James made his England A debut as a centre in the 78-6 win over Scotland in March 2003, having suffered the disappointment of missing the senior tour to Argentina the previous summer through injury. Injuries again dogged a promising career till he finally returned, playing full back in the 2004 RBS 6 Nations when he came off the bench against Ireland and starting against the All Blacks in Dunedin on the 2004 summer tour. James was one of the most impressive players at the 2005 Churchill Cup.

International Record

2002 NZ, A. 2003 W (R), It, W. 2004 I (R), NZ (1)

DID YOU KNOW?

James is the second eldest of four highly competitive brothers. His 20-year-old younger brother is a scrum half with Orrell and was in England U19s in 2003-04. Chris, three years older, has been one of the major influences in James' life and even today, James wears a sock Chris gave him every time he plays, even if he forgets to wash it. Sedbergh sports master Neil Rollings was another powerful influence on the fledgling wing at school. James calls him 'a brilliant coach'. Players he admires include Jonny Wilkinson, Jason Robinson, Carlos Spencer and Thomas Castaignede. To relax he is becoming an impressive snooker player and is a keen visitor to Cheltenham Races.

THE LIONS STORE ONLINE

WWW.LIONSRUGBY.COM

The official online store of The British & Irish Lions

A Lions Tour Dates Ball	£12.99	D Lions Midi Ball	£9.99
B Lions Replica Ball (Size 5)	£19.99	E Lions Sponge Ball	£4.99
C Lions Replica Ball (Size 4)	£19.99	F Lions Mini Ball	£4.99

G Lions No. 13 Jersey
£45.00
Available May 2005

H Lions Performance T-Shirt
£18.00

I Lions No. 10 Jersey
£45.00
Available May 2005

J Lions Training Jersey (White)
£45.00
K Lions Training Shorts (Blue)
£18.00

L Lions Home Jersey (Long Sleeve)	**£55.00**
M Lions Home Jersey (Short Sleeve)	**£50.00**
N Lions Home Junior Jersey (Short Sleeve)	**£40.00**

O Lions Press Suit
£70.00

P Lions Mug (Red)	**£4.99**
Q Lions Mug (Stipple)	**£4.99**
R Lions Mug (Blue)	**£4.99**

S Lions Tie (Stripe)	**£14.99**
T Lions Tie (Blue)	**£14.99**
U Lions Tie (Grey)	**£14.99**
V Lions Tie (Silver)	**£14.99**

W Lions Towel
£14.99

X Lions Beanie Bear
£5.99
Available April 2005

Y Lions Charlie Bear
£12.99
Available April 2005

Call 029 2034 5055 to order or visit thelionstore.com today

Prices quoted include VAT but excludes delivery charge.
Prices correct at time of going to print and are subject to availability and change.

FOUR NATIONS ONE TEAM   WWW.LIONSRUGBY.COM

OLLIE SMITH

FAST FACTS

CLUB	**Leicester Tigers**
POSITION	**Centre**
BORN	**14.8.82 Leicester**
HEIGHT	**1.85m**
WEIGHT	**96kg**
CAPS	**5**
POINTS	**0**

When Ollie Smith scored a try on his British and Irish Lions debut against Argentina it proved what a lot of people have known all along – that he's a major rugby talent. Featuring as a replacement on two occasions during the 2005 RBS 6 Nations, Ollie has been on the verge of a regular position in the England team for some seasons and could well eventually feature in the England side in his favoured position of outside centre. He is the only player ever to gain a Heineken Cup winners' medal while still a teenager and his obvious skills won him a place in England's 43-strong pre-2003 World Cup squad. He made his first test start against France in Marseille in August of 2003 in the warm-up match for what would eventually become a successful World Cup campaign. His first senior England cap, however, was when he took to the field as a 53rd minute replacement for Charlie Hodgson in the 40-5 win over Italy at Twickenham in the 2003 RBS 6 Nations. Currently at ease at centre or wing, Ollie actually sees himself as a centre who has enough pace to deliver on the wing if required. Ollie made his Leicester Tigers debut against London Irish when just 18 back in September 2000. He was the youngest player ever to come on in the Zurich Premiership at that time, though he was overtaken in May 2004 by David Doherty of Leeds Tykes. He has represented England U18s and U19s and his mixture of power and subtlety was swiftly recognised when he first appeared for England A in the match against France at Northampton in 2003. Ollie was educated at John Cleveland College, Hinckley. This season, after finally beating off a series of niggling injuries, the pacy youngster has played a key role in the improvement of Leicester Tigers and especially the renewed excellence of their back play. Having stepped up from the fringes at club level to become one of the Tigers' key players for the future, Ollie now hopes to establish himself at international level in a similar way. His experiences on the British & Irish Lions tour to New Zealand in 2005 can only help him in achieving his goals in the future.

International Record
2003 It (R), W, F 2005 It (R), S (R)

DID YOU KNOW?

Ollie plays the drums and formed a group that includes his old schoolmate and Tigers club mate, Sam Vesty on guitar. He's also finished a PE & Sports Science Degree course at Loughborough University. A Tigers man through and through, Ollie acquired his first season ticket at Welford Road at seven before joining the Tigers Academy at 16. He was nurtured by the Academy under former England centre and captain Paul Dodge. His Tigers debut remains a favourite rugby moment along with pulling on an England shirt. His biggest disappointment was missing out on a place in the England 30-man World Cup squad, having reached the last 35. When he needs to relax he picks up his rod and line and goes fishing and once caught an 18lb carp. He loves cooking and dreams of opening a restaurant one day.

MATT STEVENS

FAST FACTS

CLUB	**Bath**
POSITION	**Prop**
BORN	**1.10.82 Durban, South Africa**
HEIGHT	**1.82m**
WEIGHT	**122kg**
CAPS	**5**
POINTS	**0**

Despite often featuring as a replacement for his club side Bath, there is no doubt that there are plenty of recognised rugby experts already predicting a very bright future for Matt Stevens. His talent and skills have been picked up early by England and this year he started for his country on three occasions, against Ireland, Italy and Scotland. Matt's season was then topped off to perfection when he was selected to tour New Zealand with the Lions. Any rugby player would be delighted with such a call-up, of course, but it was a particularly thrilling moment for Matt. At 22 he's the youngest member of the party. Stevens was first brought into the England senior front row in December 2003 for the uncapped game against the New Zealand Barbarians at Twickenham, following a rib injury to the appointed captain Phil Vickery. Not only did he impress the then England Head Coach Clive Woodward with an all-round performance of power and maturity, but he also got his name on the scoresheet when he powered over for a try. A forward of immense promise who shows astonishing power in loose play, Matt was very much in demand during Bath's successful 2003-04 drive to the top of the Zurich Premiership table. In March 2004 he was then selected as a replacement for England against Ireland at Twickenham ahead of the legendary Jason Leonard. The summer tour followed and Matt earned his first two caps against the All Blacks in Dunedin and Auckland, before a knee injury made him unavailable for the test against the Wallabies in Brisbane. He is a British passport holder, but was born in Durban, South Africa, and was educated at the country's Kearsney College. Matt joined Bath in September 2002 after representing the Junior Springboks at both U18 and U19 level. His other early representative honours include playing for Western Province and South African Universities. Matt first caught the eye of the England selectors in 2003 when he was playing for England in the IRB U21 World Cup which was held in Oxfordshire that year. Gaining in experience all the time, Matt looks as if he could be an England stalwart for many years to come.

International Record
2004 NZ (1R, 2R) 2005 I, It, S

DID YOU KNOW?

Matt most admires former Bath and England player Mike Catt who is 11 years his senior. They share South African roots and both grew up in the country. Matt's family still live in South Africa, running their family game reserves and hotel business, while Matt trains in Bath and has just completed his final year there studying politics and economics. After buying a scooter down in Bath Matt found that he had a few problems getting a helmet. The trouble was that none of them would fit his rather sizeable head! He is very musical, both playing guitar and singing and he is often heard belting out a tune when he's out on tour. His other hobbies include scuba diving and also cooking. His nickname is 'Sauce'. Could it be the cooking?

MATHEW TAIT

FAST FACTS

CLUB	Newcastle Falcons
POSITION	Centre/Wing
BORN	06.02.86 County Durham
HEIGHT	1.80m
WEIGHT	80kg
CAPS	1
POINTS	0

Mathew Tait is one of the most exciting young talents to emerge through the RFU's National Academy system. Although just 19, he has become a regular in the Newcastle Falcons starting line-up and has already earned his first England cap. His impressive Premiership performances resulted in his nomination for an award by Zurich for the 2004-05 season and also for Try Of The Season against Saracens. He was also nominated for the PRA Young Player Of The Year award. In 2002 he was capped at outside centre by England U16, then U18. This was where he was spotted by the National Academy manager, Brian Ashton, who selected him for the Junior National Academy in 2003-04. Because of Ashton's belief in Tait's pace, power and eye for a gap, the 18 year old was fast-tracked straight into the Senior National Academy this season. In May 2004 he made his debut in a Zurich Premiership game against London Irish and scored a

try with his first touch of the ball. Falcons signed the centre on contract in April 2004 when he was still finishing his A-levels at Barnard Castle School. Tait played an integral part for England in the IRB U19 World Championships in South Africa in 2004 and later appeared in the winning squad that took the Dubai Sevens in December 2004. He raised many coaching eyebrows this January when he threw off a Jason Robinson tackle in a 50m run to score a superb try in Falcons' 30-29 win over Sale Sharks. His composure starting in the Falcons team for their fierce Heineken Cup match in Perpignan in the hostile atmosphere of the Stade Aime Giral just days later probably sealed his call-up to England. He also took part in the 2005 Churchill Cup, starting in the final.

International Record
2005 W

DID YOU KNOW?

Mathew played for Barnard Castle School first XV for three years under his school coach Martin Pepper, once a first class flanker with NEC Harlequins. Tait credits Pepper as being the biggest single influence on his game, but also acknowledges Rob Andrew, Brian Ashton, Falcons players such as Jonny Wilkinson and Matt Burke and the Falcons academy staff for his progress. In July 2004 he was invited to Downing Street along with talented teenagers from other sports to meet the Prime Minister, Tony Blair. His talented younger brother Alex is a full back who trains with the Falcons academy and is part of the England U18 squad. The brothers haven't played together since mini rugby days at Consett, but hope to do so for England one day. Their mother was a county sprinter and grandfather Arthur played football for Sheffield Wednesday.

STEVE THOMPSON MBE

FAST FACTS

CLUB	**Northampton Saints**
POSITION	**Hooker**
BORN	**15.7.78 Hemel Hempstead**
HEIGHT	**1.88m**
WEIGHT	**115kg**
CAPS	**39**
POINTS	**15 – 3t**

Steve Thompson is regarded by many as England's finest ever hooker and he's certainly England's biggest. Despite getting some unfair criticism from certain sections of the press, the Northampton Saints captain still left for New Zealand with the British & Irish Lions as the best hooker after playing in all five of England's 2005 RBS 6 Nations matches. He also did more than his fair share in Northampton's fight against relegation from the Zurich Premiership, a fight which they only managed to win on the very last day of a gripping season when NEC Harlequins went down. When you note that Thompson played a part in all but one of England's World Cup games in Australia in 2003, you realise how central Thompson has become to the national side. Indeed the robust but mobile hooker missed only two of England's 17 tests in 2003 and touched down for his second Test try in England's opening World Cup match against Georgia in Perth. Steve started out playing rugby at the age of 15 at the Northampton School for Boys and then went on to play for Ben Cohen's old side, Northampton Old Scouts RFC. He also trained with the youth section of Saints and, at the age of 18, was selected for the apprentice scheme at the club's Academy. Despite competing against the highly respected Argentinean Frederico Mendez in the 1999-2000 season for his club place, Steve still managed to force his way into the England A squad, including a match against Ireland A on his home Franklin's Gardens turf. Following that Steve was selected for England's summer tour to North America in 2001, where he was one of the many success stories for the national side. He scored his maiden test try against Italy in 2003 and then made a very significant contribution to England's

southern hemisphere tour in June of 2003, playing in tests against New Zealand and Australia.

International Record
2002 S, I, F, W, It, Arg, NZ, A, SA. 2003 W, It, S, I, NZ, A, F (1, 2R, 3), RWC G, SA, Sam (R), W, F, A. 2004 It, S, I ,W, F, NZ (1), A(R), C, SA, A 2005 W, F, I, It, S
Lions: 2005 (1R, 2)

DID YOU KNOW?

Steve proposed to his wife in Sydney just hours after England won the World Cup in November 2003 and just before she flew back to England. They married in the summer of 2004. When he stops playing, Steve is interested in working with underprivileged children. He singles out Mike Teague as a player he admires for being "very hard". His major influences include coach Mark Lee from school and Mat Bridge and Keith Picton from Northampton Saints' youth team, with Tim Rodber a role model as a player. Steve has two Great Danes – Geoffrey and William – who are almost as well-known as he is in Northampton, often featuring in the local media. A keen golfer, he has a 15 handicap.

MIKE TINDALL MBE

FAST FACTS

CLUB	**Gloucester**
POSITION	**Centre**
BORN	**18.10.78 Wharfedale**
HEIGHT	**1.85m**
WEIGHT	**99kg**
CAPS	**41**
POINTS	**54 – 10t, 2c**

A legend at the Rec for so long, Michael James Tindall bid farewell to Bath in 2005 despite being ruled out for much of the season with injury. A move to the club's arch rivals Gloucester next season will hopefully bring Mike more luck than he's enjoyed this term, as he's missed not only the RBS 6 Nations, but also a place on the Lions tour, despite being named in a provisional squad of 47. Nonetheless Mike can rightly be described as one of England's stalwarts. He played a critical role in all but one of England's seven World Cup matches, replacing Mike Catt in the semi-final against France, with Catt replacing him late on in the final against Australia. He first wore an England senior jersey as a 57th minute replacement in the 39-14 win over Queensland at Brisbane on the tour of Australia in June 1999, and joined the England squad as Jeremy Guscott's replacement for the 1999 Rugby World Cup quarter-final against South Africa in Paris. He marked his England starting debut with a try against Ireland at Twickenham in the opening match of the 2000 Six Nations Championship. Since then, apart from an injury that kept him out of the 2002 Investec Challenge autumn internationals, he has made the No 12 shirt more or less his own. He played a wonderful game in the 2003 Grand Slam decider against Ireland, scoring a game-breaking try. He also played a scoring role in England's 25-14 win over Australia in Melbourne during their 2003 southern hemisphere tour. An ankle injury suffered when he was playing for Bath in 2003 ruled him out of early 2004 RBS 6 Nations matches. On the 2004 Southern Hemisphere tour 'Tins' started in all three Tests and was made Vice Captain by the then England Head Coach Clive Woodward. He was educated at Queen Elizabeth Grammar School, Wakefield, represented Yorkshire Schools and played for the same England 18 Group side as Jonny Wilkinson. He became a Bath Academy player in 1997. Mike has also appeared for the Midlands & North and England at U21 level. He was named England Vice Captain in the Investec Challenge in 2004.

International Record

2000 I, F, W, It, S, SA (1, 2), A, Arg, SA. 2001 W (R), Ro, SA (R). 2002 S, I, F, W, It, NZ, A, SA. 2003 It, S, I, NZ, A, F (2), Rugby World Cup G, SA, U, W, F (R), A. 2004 W, F, NZ (1, 2) A, C, SA, A

DID YOU KNOW?

Mike is proud of starting for England in the Rugby World Cup final, of being part of England's Grand Slam victory in 2003 and of the successful southern hemisphere tour three months later. He lists the All Black captain Tana Umaga as one of his toughest opponents and feels Jeremy Guscott and England Head Coach Andy Robinson have most influenced his game, teaching him that "there's more to rugby than contact". He likes playing golf, his partner is the Queen's granddaughter, and after the 2004 summer tour acquired a young Bull Mastiff dog called Misty.

ANDY TITTERRELL

FAST FACTS

CLUB	Sale Sharks
POSITION	Hooker
BORN	10.1.81 Dartford
HEIGHT	1.80m
WEIGHT	93kg
CAPS	4
POINTS	0

There are some who might have been surprised, but it took just two England caps this season – earned from the bench in this year's RBS 6 Nations against Scotland and Italy – to get Andy Titterell booked onto the plane to the Land of the Long White Cloud with the British & Irish Lions. Sir Clive Woodward was clearly impressed by the Sale Shark. He might be small for a hooker, but there's no doubting he's a special talent. After all, Andrew forced his way into the senior England squad in 2002-03 at the tender age of just 21. He shared in England's Churchill Cup success in Canada that year, boosting his development through Sale Sharks, and was first capped for England A against Ireland A in 2002. After learning the game in Kent, Andy had spells with both Saracens and Waterloo before joining Sale Sharks back in 2001. Capped by England at both schoolboy and U21 level, he won a place in the England Elite Player Squad for 2003. It was there that Andy caught the eye of then Head Coach Clive Woodward with a dynamic display on his first start for England A against Scotland A in March 2002. He then went on to gain his second A cap against Italy A in 2003. In 2004 Andy earned England A selection against France A in their narrow defeat in Perpignan. He then took part in the 2004 senior summer tour and even managed to earn his first senior cap, coming off the bench against the All Blacks in Auckland. He added another when arriving on the Twickenham pitch as a replacement against Canada in November 2004 and after continuing to impress everyone who comes into contact with him, Titterell now seems set to challenge for a starting spot in Andy Robinson's England side going forward. Of course, it won't harm the 24-year-old's chances of making progress that he happens to be one of the fittest players in the current England squad and was called up for the Lions.

International Record
2004 NZ (2R), C (R) 2005 It (R), S (R)

DID YOU KNOW?

Andy was educated at the Hugh Christie Technology College in Tonbridge and Sevenoaks School and started playing rugby at the age of seven at the Sevenoaks club, which also nurtured England prop David Flatman and Sevens specialist Tony Roques.

At Sale Sharks he has huge respect for Brian Redpath and Jason Robinson. The biggest influences on his career to date, he says, are his throwing coaches, James Wade at the Sharks and England's Simon Hardy. His first cap while on England's 2004 summer tour against New Zealand at Eden Park is the highlight of his career to date, as well as his two uncapped England appearances against the Barbarians at Twickenham, and Sharks' Parker Pen Challenge Cup final win in 2002. He enjoys cooking for his wife Delyth, to whom he proposed as soon as he returned from the 2004 summer tour. They married in July.

SAM VESTY

FAST FACTS

CLUB	Leicester Tigers
POSITION	Fly half/Centre/Full back
BORN	26.11.81 Leicester
HEIGHT	1.83m
WEIGHT	90kg
CAPS	Uncapped

Sam is very much a homegrown Leicester talent, having started playing rugby at the Leicester Forest club (formerly Old Bosworthians) at the age of seven. His game flourished while at the John Cleveland College and he played at all representative levels in four years there, including for the England U18 Group Schools team. He was then snapped up by Leicester Tigers and graduated through their U21s and Extras. He made his first team debut in 2002, coming on as a replacement away to Biarritz Olympique. During the summer of 2002 Sam was also one of three Tigers players included in the England U21 World Cup squad that played in South Africa. With the departure of Andy Goode in the 2002-03 season and injury to Austin Healey, Sam was catapulted into the Tigers line-up and made over 20 appearances at fly half. The fans and his teammates recognised his contribution by voting him the Supporters' and the Players' Young Player of the Season. Despite the return of Goode and other signings for the 2003-04 season, his ability to play in three positions kept him very much in the first team frame and he managed 17 appearances before injury ended his season. During the 2004-05 season he again consolidated his position within the team, mainly at full back, and played over 20 games.

DID YOU KNOW?

Sam is the fourth generation of his family to don a Tigers shirt. His father Phil propped for Tigers, grandfather Bernard Albert played in the centre and his great-grandfather on his mother's side, Jack Dickens, was a Tigers wing. His introduction to rugby as an U8 was watched over by Mel Smith, late father of fellow Tiger Ollie Smith. Sam and Ollie have since teamed up in a totally different guise and play together in a four-piece band called Slo Progress (an acronym of the band members names). Sam has a Fender Strat guitar and plays rhythm, although he enjoys acoustic guitar just as much. At school he was also an extremely adept cricketer and played regularly for Leicestershire 2nd XI as wicket keeper and batsman. He also played tennis at county level and today enjoys a game of golf whenever he can, playing off an 18 handicap. He says his John Cleveland sports coach Paul Walsh taught him what rugby was all about, while Tigers coach Pat Howard has also had a great influence on his career. Away from the pitch, he enjoys relaxing with his young son Harry George and partner Katie.

The Perfect All-rounder

"Whatever level you play at, the Concept 2 Indoor Rower can help you in your training. For developing and maintaining cardiovascular endurance it has the advantage of exercising all the major muscle groups of the body, spreading the workload throughout the musculature, so making it possible to work at relatively high levels of intensity while maintaining a comfortable level of stress on the cardiovascular system. Local muscular endurance is also developed throughout the main muscles and not just restricted to specific muscle groups.

"Its non-impact nature and smooth motion reduces the risk of soft tissue and overuse injuries, common in other training modes, to miniscule levels. The Performance Monitor, meanwhile, makes it simple to execute many different types of training sessions including intervals and fartlek. It also offers accurate assessment of work rate while training and exact volumes and workloads at the end of sessions, which is crucial when following a long-term training programme.

"Having trained on the Concept 2 Indoor Rower consistently for the past 12 years it is the one machine that has stood the test of time. For my players it adds an invaluable dimension to their training, while for me a daily 30-40 minute workout on the Indoor Rower while watching TV must be the simplest and most enjoyable way of keeping fit for life."

Eddie O'Sullivan

To find out more about the Concept 2 Indoor Rower, visit **www.concept2.co.uk** or call **0115 945 5522**.

Eddie O'Sullivan - Irish & British Lions Coach

PHIL VICKERY MBE

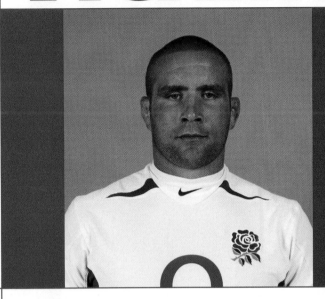

FAST FACTS

CLUB	**Gloucester**
POSITION	**Prop**
BORN	**14.3.76 Barnstaple**
HEIGHT	**1.90m**
WEIGHT	**109kg**
CAPS	**45**
POINTS	**5 – 1t**

A start against France in 2005 followed a spot on the bench against Wales and it seemed that Phil Vickery's injury problems were finally behind him. Not so. He broke his arm playing against Bath and was ruled out for the rest of the season. Tough break – literally. Still, Phil Vickery is one of the most respected props in the world, despite some long absences in his career due to his many and varied injuries. His brief comeback in 2005 began with Gloucester just into the New Year when he played a full match against Leicester. He was a rock for England on the road to the 2003 World Cup success, playing in all seven games in the tournament and captaining the side against Uruguay. He scored his first try in international rugby when he came off the bench against Samoa in England's third game of the 2003 World Cup.

A proud Cornishman from farming stock, Phil made his test debut against Wales in 1998 to complete an exraordinarily rapid rise to prominence after only 34 first team games for his club and just 81 days after he made his England A debut. But Philip John Vickery has been dogged by injury throughout his career. His started with Bude, the Cornish club, then moved to Redruth, from where he first appeared in an England Colts side. Having graduated to Gloucester, the injury problems began. He recovered from a neck injury in April 1999 and played in that year's Rugby World Cup. A shoulder injury, however, kept him out of the 2000 South Africa tour. Vickery's honest work in the tight and mobility in the loose helped him win a place on the 2001 Lions tour of Australia, where he appeared in all three tests. He also captained an unfancied and inexperienced England side to victory against Argentina in Buenos Aries in 2002, but was forced to miss the entire 2002-03

RBS 6 Nations Championship after sustaining a back injury in training that required an operation. A rib injury scuppered plans by then England Head Coach Clive Woodward to make him England captain in the non-capped match against the New Zealand Barbarians in December 2003. Although he took a full part in the 2004 RBS 6 Nations, another back operation in May ruled him out of the summer tour to New Zealand and Australia.

International Record
1998 W, A (2), NZ (1, 2), SA. 1999 USA, C, World Cup: It, NZ, Tg, SA. 2000 I, F, W, S, A, Arg (R), SA,(R). 2001 W, It, S, A, SA. 2002 I, F, Arg, NZ, A, SA. 2003 NZ, A, Rugby World Cup G, SA, Sam (R), U, W, F, A. 2004 It, S, I, W, F. 2005 W (R), F Lions: 2001 A (1, 2, 3)

DID YOU KNOW?

Phil's roots are firmly in Cornwall, which he describes as an "awesome place". He was educated at Bude Haven Secondary School, Cornwall and he remembers his first sporting honour as playing for Cornwall Under 16s. Even his sporting heroes are local, with Cornwall and Redruth prop Richard Keast topping the list. He thinks he would have become a farmer if he hadn't become a professional rugby player.

TOM VOYCE

PLAYER PROFILE

FAST FACTS

CLUB	**London Wasps**
POSITION	**Wing/Full back**
BORN	**05.01.81 Truro**
HEIGHT	**1.85m**
WEIGHT	**94kg**
CAPS	**3**
POINTS	**0**

Thomas Michael Dunstan Voyce is one of the cutting edges in attack for London Wasps, which he ably demonstrated in 2005 when scoring a blistering try in their winning Zurich Premiership final against Leicester Tigers when he sprinted 50m unopposed. He was born in Truro and educated at Penair School. From there he went on to study at King's School, Taunton, and eventually embarked on an unfinished course at the Royal Agriculture College, Cirencester.

He had first shown promise playing mini rugby at Penryn RFC, before going on to play for Truro RFC U15s and U16s. Having left Cornwall at 16, Tom eventually joined Bath where he worked his way through the club's lower sides and into the Zurich Premiership line-up. He was also selected for England's 2001 tour to North America, where he won his first cap against the USA. In 2003 he moved to London to join London Wasps for the 2003-04 season and quickly established himself as a first team regular. He played in 34 of his club's 35 matches that season, scoring 15 tries in the process. In November 2004 he scored the quickest try in Premiership history when he gathered a loose ball from kick off and crossed by the posts in 9.63 seconds against NEC Harlequins, beating the Premiership record of Leicester Tiger's Martin Corry by some 14 seconds. Tom was in the starting line up for the 2004 England summer tour matches against New Zealand in Auckland and Australia in Brisbane. Tom was top try scorer in the 2005 Churchill Cup.

International Record
2001 USA. 2004 NZ (2), A

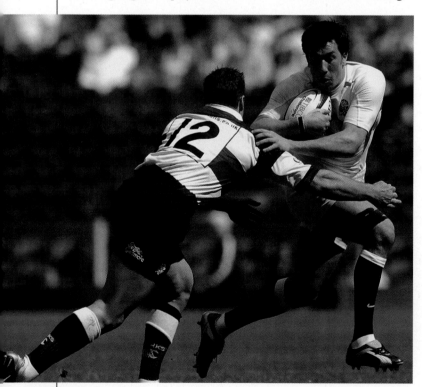

DID YOU KNOW?

Tom's great uncle, Thomas Anthony Voyce, won 24 caps for England, 23 as a flanker and one on the wing during the 1920s and went on to become President of the RFU in 1960-61. His great uncle was a member of the first double Grand Slam winning team. Now living in Richmond with wife Nicole, Tom's hobbies include a passion for shooting. He goes to the West Wycombe shooting ground to practise, close to London Wasps' base at the Causeway Stadium, and also on some game shoots. His other pastimes include golf, while his musical tastes vary from the Black Eyed Peas to the jazz of Jamie McCullum.

HUGH VYVYAN

FAST FACTS

CLUB	Saracens
POSITION	Lock/No. 8
BORN	08.08.76 Guildford
HEIGHT	1.98m
WEIGHT	102kg
CAPS	1
POINTS	5 – 1t

Hugh is a powerful and highly mobile forward and a proven leader. He won a deserved first cap against Canada in the Investec Challenge match in November 2004 and scored a try in front of the Twickenham crowd. As well as captaining both Newcastle Falcons and now Saracens, he also captained England A in February to their victory over France A and the England squad on the previous two Churchill Cup tours. The first in 2003 saw England take the Cup and last year saw England losing to the New Zealand Maori in extra time. In 2002 he toured with the full England side and was an unused bench replacement against Argentina. In that same 2002-03 season he played for England A against Scotland A and Ireland A and, in December 2003, also helped an England XV beat the New Zealand Barbarians.

Hugh opted to take a year out after Downside School and played in South Africa for the Villagers club in Cape Town. Once back in England he played briefly for Penryn before starting a successful theology degree at Newcastle University, where he caught the eye of the Falcons and eventually made his debut against Moseley, when the club was in National Division 2. In 2001 he was an important member of Falcons' Powergen Cup-winning side at Twickenham, a feat he repeated in 2004 at Twickenham, before moving to Saracens where he was made captain before even having played a game. Hugh missed this years Churchill Cup through injury and was replaced by Phil Dowson.

International Record
C (R)

DID YOU KNOW?

Hugh's middle name is Donnithorne, an old Cornish name given to him by his father, who had also christened each of his six elder brothers and sister in a similar manner. The Vyvyan dynasty has even turned out its own sevens team at the Penryn Sevens, making the final on four occasions and winning it twice. The former England full back and now Academy coach Jon Callard heavily influenced Hugh's early career while at Downside School, moving him from fly half to No 8. Brother Charlie was a No 8 for Sale Sharks and was another big influence on his career. Hugh has set up his own company, CHV Sporting, concentrating on corporate hospitality, in partnership with Chris Hattam, the best man at his wedding.

MICKY WARD

FAST FACTS

CLUB	Newcastle Falcons
POSITION	Prop
BORN	09.01.79 Wallsend
HEIGHT	1.80m
WEIGHT	119kg
CAPS	Uncapped

A canny Geordie and a diehard Falcon, Micky was briefly called into the England squad for the RBS 6 Nations. He caught the rugby bug while at Burnside High School and joined Wallsend rugby club when he was 13. He made his representative debut in the Northumberland Schools U16 side and it was while playing for the U17s that he was picked up by the Falcons' Paul Mackinnon to join their Academy. He toured Argentina with England U19s and returned there with the England U21s on his second SANZAR competition, having also played in New Zealand. He was also a member of England's 2004 Churchill Cup squad and came off the bench in both matches against Canada and the New Zealand Maori. Micky made his Falcons debut against Bath in the old Cheltenham & Gloucester Cup and has now made over 150 appearances for them – he's a living legend amongst the Kingston Park faithful. He has just signed another two-year contract with the club.

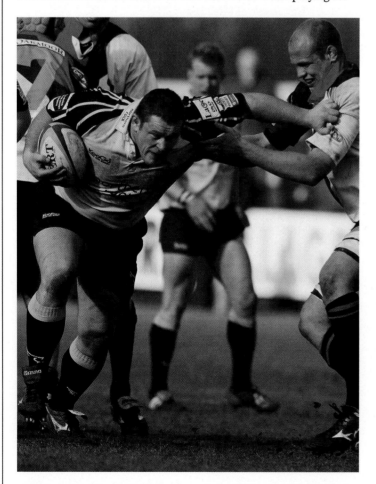

DID YOU KNOW?

Micky's father, Dickie Ward, is a builder and Micky followed in his footsteps, having already renovated and sold on two houses in Wallsend. He enjoys doing the plumbing and electrics, but leaves the gas to someone else. Having left school at 17, his father got him a job delivering soft drinks as well as getting him to help out in his own business as a jack-of-all-trades. However, he was always allowed time off for his training and matches and owes his father a great debt of gratitude for that. Signing the contract with the Falcons is still one of the highlights of his career, along with his Churchill Cup and two Tetley Cup final appearances. Micky rates Jason Leonard as the player who's made the greatest impression on him, both on and off the field. When he's not at Kingston Park, he loves to help coach the Wallsend 1st XV and is looking to continue coaching when he finally retires from playing.

LOVE RUGBY!

WORLD CLASS MUSEUM & STADIUM TOUR

STOP PRESS ... Webb Ellis trophy on show until **21st November** – don't miss it!

DISCOVER A WHOLE WORLD OF RUGBY AT TWICKENHAM

Celebrate the game worldwide ... at the home of England Rugby on a Stadium Tour & Museum visit!

plus ... The Rugby Store
UK's largest supplier of official England Rugby merchandise. Phone 0870 405 2003 or visit www.rfu.com **OPEN 7 DAYS A WEEK**

plus ... The Scrummery Café Bar
OPEN 6 DAYS A WEEK   07947 414695

www.rfu.com/microsites/museum

Only 20 minutes by train from central London!

• Group discounts • Exclusive tours with corporate hospitality • Supporters Club discount 2 for 1 • Gift vouchers
• Exhibitions • World's largest rugby reference library available
• School packs • Wheelchair access

TWICKENHAM
STADIUM TOURS & MUSEUM OF RUGBY

Twickenham East Stand, Rugby Road, Twickenham TW1 1DZ
Phone 0870 405 2001 NOW
for opening times and bookings

FREE PARKING

JULIAN WHITE MBE

FAST FACTS

CLUB	Leicester Tigers
POSITION	Prop
BORN	14.5.73 Plymouth
HEIGHT	1.85m
WEIGHT	119kg
CAPS	28
POINTS	0

Although making just one solitary appearance in the 2005 RBS 6 Nations, against Wales, Julian White is now considered to be England's form tight-head. He is regarded as one of the most powerful forwards in the game and demonstrated it when playing outstandingly in England's three tests in the autumn of 2004. Julian was part of the England World Cup squad in Australia, where he was in the starting line-up against Samoa and came on as replacement against Uruguay. In 2004, with Phil Vickery recovering from a back operation, Julian grasped the chance to demonstrate his formidable scrummaging skills in the England front row during the RBS 6 Nations and the summer tour to the southern hemisphere. He had made his senior international breakthrough at tighthead in the two tests against South Africa on the 2000 tour, having first played for England A against Ireland A at Northampton earlier that year.

White joined Saracens from Bridgend in 1999 and swiftly made his Premiership debut in the 28-23 defeat of London Irish at Vicarage Road, Watford on the opening weekend of the season. As a youngster he played mini and junior rugby for Salcombe and had played in the same senior side as his father, a former Plymouth Albion player. He served his rugby apprenticeship with Okehampton and Plymouth Albion and had a spell in New Zealand with Hawkes Bay and Canterbury Crusaders. He appeared in his first Twickenham test against Argentina in November 2001, playing until half time when he was replaced by Phil Vickery. He toured North America in the summer of 2001, forming a solid front row with Graham Rowntree and Dorian West. At the start of the 2002 season he transferred back to the West Country with Bristol Shoguns, but joined Leicester Tigers for the 2003-04 season following the relegation of Bristol Shoguns from the Premiership. After an operation on his knee, Julian returned to the England squad in the 2004 RBS 6 Nations when he came off the bench against Wales and France. He appeared in all three Lions tests against New Zealand in 2005.

International Record

2000 SA (1, 2), Arg, SA, 2001 F, C (1, 2), USA, I, Ro. 2002 S, W, It. 2003 W, F (1 ,2, 3), RWC Sam, U (R). 2004 W (R), F (R), NZ (1, 2), Aus, C, SA, A. 2005 W
Lions: 2005 (1, 2, 3)

DID YOU KNOW?

Julian has already bought some land in his beloved Devon and when his playing days are over, he plans to become a beef and sheep farmer. He gets back to Devon whenever he can, along with his girlfriend and two dogs, Buster, a Jack Russell, and Digger, an energetic Australian cattle dog. He also likes getting out in the fresh air on his Triumph 1000 motorbike. He says a prop's job is simply to bend down and push, although those that have come up against him can testify to how well he fulfils the requirement.

JONNY
WILKINSON OBE

FAST FACTS

CLUB	**Newcastle Falcons**
POSITION	**Fly half**
BORN	**25.5.79 Frimley**
HEIGHT	**1.77m**
WEIGHT	**86kg**
CAPS	**52**
POINTS	**817 – 5t, 123c, 161pg, 21dg**

First it was the 'Will-he, won't he?' saga for England, then it was the same again for the Lions and, while he didn't manage to return for his country this season, he did make it in time for the British & Irish Lions after putting together a handful of strong performances for Newcastle at the tail end of the season. Jonathan Peter Wilkinson OBE indelibly etched his name into rugby folklore on November 22nd, 2003, when his extra time drop goal sailed between Sydney's Telstra Stadium posts to seal England's historic 20-17 win over Australia in the Rugby World Cup final. He is unquestionably one of the most famous, modest and hard working sporting figures in the world. During the 2003 World Cup he won his 50th cap in the 28-17 win over Wales. He had been successful with all seven of his kicks against Georgia and scored all of England's points in their 24-7 victory over France in the semi-final. He was the leading points scorer ahead of Frederic Michalak of France and Australia's Elton Flatley. Although injured for most of the months following the World Cup, Jonny made his club comeback at the start of the 2004-05 season and was appointed England captain in October 2004. A new setback came in October after he took a heavy hit on his upper arm from Joe Worsley in club play. Once back in full flight in January, he then injured his left knee against Perpignan. Earlier in his career he set an individual Six Nations points scoring record with his 35 points against Italy at Twickenham in 2001, to overtake the record of his Newcastle Falcons boss, Rob Andrew. He scored all 15 points as England beat New Zealand 15-13 in Wellington 2003 and was a major factor in the 25-14 win over Australia a week later. He won his first cap at 18 and toured South Africa with England in 2000, kicking all of the points in their 27-22 win in Bloemfontein. Jonny was the first choice fly half for the 2001 Lions tour to Australia, where he equalled the Lions best individual points total in a test, with 18 points.

International Record
1998 I (R), A, NZ (1) 1999 S, I, F, W, A, USA, C World Cup It, NZ, Fj, SA (R) 2000 I, F, W, It, S, SA (2), A, Arg, SA 2001 W, It, S, F, I, A, SA 2002 S, I, F, W, It, NZ, A, SA 2003 F (1&3), W, It, S, I, NZ, A, RWC G, SA, Sam, W, F, A Lions: 2001 A (1, 2, 3), 2005 NZ (1, 2)

DID YOU KNOW?

Jonny was educated at Pierrepont in Frensham and Lord Wandsworth College in Hampshire, having started playing rugby as a four year old at Farnham RFC. His father, Phil, has been the biggest influence in his rugby career. Jonny admires Jonathan Davies for his skills and ability to switch codes, Grant Fox for his kicking, his Falcons boss Rob Andrew, and Ellery Hanley from Rugby league. His tip for success is to work hard and set challenging goals. In his spare time he enjoys being with his family and learning to play guitar.

JOE WORSLEY MBE

FAST FACTS

CLUB	**London Wasps**
POSITION	**Flanker**
BORN	**14.6.77 London**
HEIGHT	**1.95m**
WEIGHT	**111kg**
CAPS	**44**
POINTS	**45 – 9t**

Joe Paul Richard Worsley is now a vital member of England's back row, having cemented a place in Head Coach Andy Robinson's side. He played in every one of England's 2005 RBS 6 Nations games and really made his mark when he crossed the whitewash for a try against Scotland in England's last match of the tournament.

A star for his country against both South Africa and Australia in November 2004, Joe is now an automatic choice after former captain Lawrence Dallaglio retired from England duty. Joe was a member of England's victorious Rugby World Cup squad in 2003, coming on during the pool match against South Africa and starting against both Samoa and Uruguay. It crowned a marvellous year for him. He scored England's second try in their win over Wales at Cardiff earlier in the year, just eight days after scoring against France A for England A at Northampton, and being voted 'Man of the Match'. Joe was first capped against Tonga in the 1999 Rugby World Cup, then came on as a replacement against both Scotland and Italy during England's Six Nations Championship matches in 2000. He won two more caps as a replacement in that summer's tests against South Africa in Pretoria and Bloemfontein. He then enjoyed a successful tour to North America in the summer of 2001, filling Lawrence Dallaglio's No 8 position and scoring against both Canada and the United States. He continued in the back row for England's 2001 Investec Challenge matches when he turned in two outstanding performances against both Australia and South Africa. Joe also replaced Richard Hill in both of England's 2003 tour matches against New Zealand and Australia. In 2004 he played against Italy, Ireland and France in the RBS 6 Nations Championship, as well as coming off the bench against Wales to score a match-winning try. He was an important member of the brilliant London Wasps side that won both the Zurich Premiership final and the Heineken European Cup Final in 2004 and he further established his international credentials with some fine performances on England's summer tour to New Zealand and Australia. Joe again won the Zurich Premiership final with Wasps when they beat Leicester Tigers in 2005.

International Record:

1999 RWC Tg, Fj 2000 It (R), S (R), SA (1R, 2R) 2001 It (R), S (R), F (R), C (1, 2), USA, A, Ro, SA 2002 S, I, F, W (R), Arg 2003 W (R), It, S (R), I (R), NZ (R), A (R), W, RWC SA (R), Sam, U 2004 It, I, W (R), F, NZ (1R, 2) A, SA, A 2005 W, F, I, It, S

DID YOU KNOW?

If Joe hadn't taken up rugby he believes he would have swapped a No 8 on the pitch for rowing eights on the river. He names Sir Steve Redgrave as an influence on his sporting development. In his spare time Joe likes to relax by playing the piano. He was educated at Hitchin Boys School and Brunel University and joined London Wasps at the age of 16 from Welwyn Garden City RFC. He became the youngest player to represent England U21s after being a member of the England Schools 18 Group Grand Slam team in 1994-95.

MIKE WORSLEY

FAST FACTS

CLUB	NEC Harlequins
POSITION	Prop
BORN	1.12.76 Warrington
HEIGHT	1.83m
WEIGHT	110kg
CAPS	3
POINTS	0

M ike Worsley – no relation to his namesake Joe – won his first England cap as a replacement in their 40-5 win over Italy at Twickenham in March 2003. His performance against France A that year led to his RBS 6 Nations appearance, taking over from Robbie Morris in the second half. He was then included on England's pre-World Cup tour to New Zealand and played against the New Zealand Maori. He came off the bench against Australia in Brisbane during England's 2004 tour, flying there with London Wasps prop Will Green straight from the Churchill Cup tour. This year he joined England on the eve of their final Six Nations game against Scotland, after an injury to Graham Rowntree in training during the captain's run. He replaced Duncan Bell in the second half

of England's 43-22 victory over the Scots, earning his third cap.

Mike started out with the West Park St Helen's club and found representative honours with the England Schools 16 and 18 Group teams and England U21s. He had spells with Orrell and Bristol before joining London Irish in September 1998 and was a member of the Exiles' Powergen Cup-winning team of 2002. His first England A appearance was against France in Redruth 2001 and his injury against the Barbarians denied him his third tour with England for the Churchill Cup. He joined NEC Harlequins for the 2003-04 season.

International Record
2003 It (R) 2004 A (R) 2005 S (R)

DID YOU KNOW?

Mike has a law degree from the University of the West of England, Bristol, and may well return to law when his playing days are over. While studying for his degree he found the travelling between Bristol and Orrell was affecting his studies too much and so, for his final year, he joined Bristol for a season before moving to London Irish. At his St. Ambrose College, Altrincham school, he had also been a field athlete competing in the shot putt for Greater Manchester. While at London Irish, former South African coach Brendan Venter had a great influence on his career. Their Powergen Cup win over Northampton Saints was one of the highlights of his playing career, as well as his England appearances. He also enjoyed another highlight when he returned to Irish's Madejski Stadium base in Reading as a member of the NEC Harlequins Parker Pen Challenge Cup side that beat Montferrand in the exciting 2004 final by 27 points to 26.

THE
MANAGEMENT

ANDY ROBINSON OBE England Head Coach

Andy Robinson took over as Acting England Head Coach in September 2004 and six weeks later was confirmed in the post until 2008. He was brought into the England set-up by Sir Clive Woodward in May 2000 to replace the New Zealander John Mitchell. Woodward and Robinson had already shared a highly successful coaching partnership at England U21 level and at Bath. He taught Maths and PE at Colston's Collegiate in Bristol and King Edwards in Bath and joined Bath as a player in 1986. One year later, flanker Robinson won his first cup final. In 1988 he earned his first England cap in the 28-8 defeat against Australia in Sydney. In 1992, as captain, he led Bath to a league and cup double and in total he won six championships and nine cups with his club. In 1996 he left teaching and playing to become Assistant Coach at Bath and was soon known as a tactician and motivator. By 1997 he had been promoted to Chief Coach, with Clive Woodward as his backs coach. He coached Bath to European Cup success in 1998 in a thrilling 19-18 victory over Brive in Bordeaux, the country's first European champions in the Heineken Cup. In 2001 he was deputy to chief Lions coach Graham Henry for their tour to Australia and was also part of Clive Woodward's coaching team for this summer's Lions tour to New Zealand.

DAVE ALRED MBE England Assistant Coach

Dave Alred is regarded as one of the finest kicking coaches in the international game. He was a trusted lieutenant of Sir Clive Woodward in the 2003 World Cup campaign, with Woodward also paying tribute to Alred's team role in the field of mental preparation. He enjoyed a first-class playing career, playing at Bristol as full back, then at Bath, before moving to experience a new culture with three years in American Football as a kicker with the Minnesota Vikings. He started coaching rugby in 1984 with a GB Rugby League squad that included Joe Lydon, now a fellow England coach. In the early nineties he coached at Bath, when Andy Robinson was captain. Alred was then involved with the Wallabies and with England's fly half Rob Andrew, who's used him at Newcastle Falcons since his own retirement as a player. Alred now works closely with England Head Coach Andy Robinson and renewed his association with Clive Woodward on the Lions tour this summer as part of Woodward's coaching team.

PHIL LARDER MBE England Assistant Coach

Phil Larder is regarded as one of the finest defensive coaches in the game and one of the most successful "crossovers", as his union coaching career came after many seasons in the league code where he also reached the top of his profession. In the 2003 World Cup and in all their recent triumphs, England's miserly defence has been at the heart of the team's success. Larder started his rugby career in rugby union, playing for a strong Loughborough Colleges side before moving to play at Broughton Park, Manchester and Sale. In 1968 he turned professional and switched codes to rugby league when he joined Oldham. He started coaching in 1982 and became Assistant Coach to the Great Britain rugby league team in 1985. A decade later, he had control of the Great Britain team in the 1996 Rugby League World Cup. He made the switch to union in 1998 when he was recruited by Clive Woodward to specialise in England's defence. He was appointed to the coaching team for Graham Henry's Lions tour in 2001 and was one of the coaches for this summer's Lions tour to New Zealand under Woodward.

JOE LYDON England Assistant Coach

Joe Lydon is one of the most famous players in rugby league history. He joined the England coaching team full time in May 2004 under Clive Woodward and now has special responsibility for the backs and for restoring attacking dimensions to the squad. He served a fine apprenticeship in union after his switch from league. He began with the England U19 team, then became coach of the England sevens team in 2001. During his time in charge England won the Hong Kong Sevens in 2002, 2003 and 2004 and finished second overall in the 2002-03 IRB World Sevens Series. His rugby league honours include 32 Great Britain caps, seven championships, five Challenge Cups, three Premiership trophies and two World Club Championship winners' medals. In 1996 Joe moved from being manager at Wigan to become the RFL's first ever Technical Director. He switched to the RFU in September 2000 and was a coach for the 2003 RBS 6 Nations Championship, as well as the England Sevens team. This summer he was coach to the Churchill Cup winning squad.

MOVING FORWARD

Coach Mike Friday will be pleased with much of England's sevens season, but he will also be convinced his team can better their performances in the next campaign...

WORDS: JIM BYERS

The England Sevens squad will look back on their most recent campaign with mixed emotions. Coach Mike Friday's men launched their assault on the IRB Series in confident fashion with an impressive victory at the circuit's first event in Dubai back in December. But that early triumph was not to be repeated in any of the six events that followed in the season and England finished the series in third place in the IRB rankings after being edged out of second spot by Fiji at the final event in Paris in June.

Positive strides were made in terms of blooding new players, with the likes of youngsters Mathew Tait, Delon Armitage, Will Matthews and Will Skirving all getting

Below:
Ollie Phillips scores against Tunisia in South Africa

Right:
Pat Sanderson celebrates sevens victory in Dubai

valuable experience of world class sevens action. And there were some fine individual achievements too, notably from Ben Gollings, who overtook Fiji legend Waisale Serevi at the top of the IRB's all-time points list at the Wellington event. It was also a memorable season for paceman Richard Haughton, who bagged his 100th sevens try at the Paris event. But given England's traditional strength in sevens rugby, they will look back on the season believing they could have achieved even more.

After seeing off Fiji in a pulsating final at the first event in Dubai, England then fell at the semi-final stages of the next competition in George, South Africa. This time it was Fiji who won, gaining revenge over an England side that had narrowly avoided defeat to Scotland in the pool stages and was having to perform without talismanic playmaker Simon Amor, injured in the Dubai final.

In February's competition down in Wellington, New Zealand, England again fell short against Fiji, this time losing 24-19 in the quarterfinals of the main cup competition. And worse was to follow as Friday's outfit slumped to a painful 19-17 defeat to Scotland in the semi-final of the plate.

Over in Los Angeles for the American leg of the series, England bowed out in the semi-finals, this time against an impressive Argentina side, while at the World Cup Sevens in Hong Kong in March England were massively unlucky to go out to eventual winners Fiji in a pulsating semi.

At April's Singapore event the team ended their winless run against Fiji by beating the South Sea Islanders in a storming semi-final thanks to a last-gasp try from that man Gollings. But clearly tired after such exertions, the heat and humidity told against England in the final, where they lost to New Zealand by 26 points to 5.

England attempted to retain their crown at the penultimate competition in London, but Friday's side, which had lost to Samoa in a pool game, were unfortunately beaten in the final by a powerful South African outfit.

The Springboks then repeated the feat at the final tournament in Paris, this time in the Plate final after England lost in the quarter-finals of the main competition to Samoa.

Plenty of positives can be taken from England's sevens season, but a third place finish is something Mike Friday will believe his team can improve on next season.

TOUGH TIMES

With England's Under 21s landing the Grand Slam last season, this year's crop of youngsters certainly had plenty to live up to. But the squad, led by National Academy coaches Jim Mallinder and Nigel Redman and team manager Peter Drewett, endured a somewhat disappointing campaign in terms of results, if not performances. The season was also overshadowed by a serious neck injury to prop Matt Hampson. The Leicester Tigers player suffered the tragic accident in training

Far Right:
Tom Varndell
makes his
mark against
Samoa in
the IRB
U21 World
Championships

Right:
England's
David
Seymour on
the charge
against
Scotland

prior to March's Six Nations match against Scotland and is still in Stoke Mandeville Hospital.

The 21s' season got underway in November with two annual representative fixtures at Marcoussis in France. In what were effectively trial matches ahead of the Six Nations, England North beat France East 22-25 before France West narrowly squeezed out England South 17-7. The real action kicked off in February, however, when England launched the defence of their Six Nations trophy against Wales. Unfortunately, Mallinder's side, with many still qualifying for this age group next season, didn't get the start they'd hoped for with a 32-21 defeat at Rodney Parade. And there was further

agony against France in the next match as the U21s were denied the win they deserved by a last-minute try which sent them to a 20-17 defeat at Franklin's Gardens in Northampton, their designated 'home ground' for the season. The squad's confidence was restored after a determined side ran in five tries against Ireland in a 28-6 win, before landing a second victory of the season with a hard-fought 31-14 victory over Italy.

The Six Nations campaign ended on a sad note after Matt Hampson's tragic accident in the lead-up to the Scotland game. But the match went ahead as a tribute and with the blessing of Matt's family. The England players carried the initials MH embroidered under the

red rose on their jerseys as a gesture of support for their team mate. After a tight contest at Northampton, England were eventually edged out 19-17 after the Scots slotted a penalty two minutes from time.

At June's IRB U21 World Championships in Argentina, England entered the event as seventh seeds, looking to bounce back from their Six Nations disappointment and also to improve on the fifth place finish at the previous year's event in Scotland. Despite a classy win over Samoa in their first match, the youngsters were out-muscled by a typically aggressive South African side in the next game before falling to a well-drilled France outfit. Defeat to hosts Argentina followed, before the side ended the tournament on a heroic high for the Under 21s with an absolutely terrific eight-try, 57-32 win over Six Nations champions Wales in the final match of the Championships.

Despite the inconsistent results over the course of the season, several England players distinguished themselves during the campaign. Chief amongst them were ponytailed Saracens flanker David Seymour and powerful Worcester No 8 Mark Hopley who were fearless in attack and defence. Behind the scrum Falcons fly half Toby Flood did an excellent job of directing the play and kicking the points, while Gloucester's elusive and skillful full back Olly Morgan won widespread praise for some solid all-round performances.

UNDER 21S

STEPPING UP

England's Under 19s had a fine season, completing a memorable Grand Slam and making a big impression at the World Championships

The Under 19s reigned supreme in the UK during their 2005 campaign, but fell just short when it came to challenging their counterparts from the Southern Hemisphere. The future looks bright for English rugby, however, after this talented crop of youngsters stormed their way to a first ever Grand Slam win at this age-group level. Those to catch the eye along the way included captain Jordan Crane, the impressive Leeds Tykes back row forward, and stand off Daniel Cipriani, of Wasps who's been fast-tracked through the RFU's Academy coaching system.

The England youngsters, led by Coaches Tosh Askew and World Cup-winning hooker Dorian West, commenced their Six Nations challenge in February with a 24-10 victory over Wales at Aberavon. They then made it two from two after a gritty 18-12 win over France in stormy conditions at Doncaster's Castle Park. A try each for pacy wingman Dominic Waldouck and skipper Crane, plus a conversion and penalty from Cipriani, earned the victory. The following week Scotland ran Askew's side extremely close at the Myreside ground in Edinburgh, but the men in white dug deep and finally emerged with a hard-fought 18-6 win.

The Under 19s' 100% record was maintained in fine style away in Blackrock, Dublin, as Askew and West's troops dished out a heavy 47-6 beating to Ireland, before England notched up their historic Grand Slam victory on home turf in Doncaster with an emphatic 50-8, eight try romp against Italy.

In April, a 26-strong Under 19 party headed off to the IRB World

Championships in Durban, South Africa. Their first two games produced wins over Japan and Scotland, but the team's superb run was finally halted after a 24-17 defeat to a powerful New Zealand side.

A loser's bonus point earned England a semi-final spot against hosts and favourites South Africa, but they were out-muscled in a physical encounter which ended in a close 17-12 defeat. The youngsters eventually ended up with a fourth place finish after being edged out 29-21 by a competitive Australian side in the third/fourth play-offs.

Reflecting on the campaign, Askew said, "We're stepping up all the time and I'm sure in the next year or two we'll be beating the likes of Australia, South Africa and New Zealand."

WORDS: JIM BYERS

Above:
Under 19s skipper Jordan Crane takes on South Africa

Left:
Dominic Waldouck scores against Japan

DOUBLE GLORY

The prospect of two major tournaments at the same time did nothing to faze an outstanding crop of England Under 18s

Below left:
Alex Tait,
brother of
Mathew, was
a key member
of the Under
18s Four
Nations team

Below right:
Tom Jokelson,
who led
England to
AER victory

With the Four Nations Championships in Wales overlapping with a European Tournament in France, two England Under 18 squads were dispatched in a bid for double glory. At the Association Européen Rugby (AER) Festival, the England side eased to a 21-3 win over Romania in their first game, before dispatching Italy 20-11 to make the final. The England young guns then emerged victorious from a tight contest with top seeds and trophy holders France. A second-half try from hooker Ross McMillan gave England a deserved 16-9 triumph, as well as revenge for last year's 32-0 mauling at the same stage.

Meanwhile, back in the UK, the 'other' England Under 18s squad gathered to do battle with Scotland, Ireland and Wales in the Four Nations tournament. Previously, England fielded a team consisting entirely of Under 18 club players at the Home Unions event, but this year it was a combined schools and clubs squad, following a restructuring of schools and youth rugby.

The first match against Scotland produced a comprehensive 48-13 win, with Barnard Castle and Durham full back Alex Tait, younger brother of England international and sevens star Mathew, scoring two of his side's seven tries.

Defeat followed as the youngsters crashed to a 20-6 loss against Wales in dreadful, mud-soaked conditions at Dunvant's Broadacre ground. But coach Alan Hughes' side bounced back to end their Four Nations efforts with a morale-boosting 38-19 victory over their Irish counterparts.

Following the defeat to Wales, England required Scotland to beat the Welsh. This seemed unlikely; Wales had won the previous six Four Nations events. In the end the Scots couldn't oblige, but they did hold Wales to an unexpected 6-6 draw, leaving England to share the title with the men in red.

One Under 18 squad member who should be especially commended for his efforts is lock Sam McDonald (RGS Worcester and Worcester Warriors), who was the only player to be involved in both the Four Nations and AER squads. McDonald played in all England's games in the AER competition and was then drafted into the Four Nations squad to play as a late replacement in the match against Ireland.

WORDS: JIM BYERS PICS: GLOUCESTERSHIRE PICTURE AGENCY

UNDER 18S

A FINE CAMPAIGN

England's women performed well all through their season and were only robbed of Six Nations glory at the death...

England's women enjoyed another superb season, marred only by a single, injury-time defeat to France in the Six Nations, which scuppered hopes of retaining the championship trophy.

Following a series of trial matches in October and November, the campaign kicked off with two autumn internationals against Canada. With injuries affecting Head Coach Geoff Richards' team selection, a number of younger players including Charlotte Barras and Vicki Massarella were handed chances to impress in the first Canada clash. Led by captain Paula George, the team recorded a comfortable 45-5 win in the first game at Richmond. And it was a similar story in the second fixture at Newbury as Richards' side eased to a 41-3 win, Barras scoring a try in only her second game for her country.

In December England A took on Wales at Clifton in a non-cap international. Richards used the opportunity to blood more youngsters, with Thirsk Sharks' 17-year-old centre Michaela Staniford, who shone in the trials, making her first England start. With captain Susie Appleby scoring two of England's eight tries, Wales fell to a comprehensive 50-17 defeat.

The first game of the Six Nations saw England take on Wales again, this time at Cardiff Arms Park. Led by Worcester scrum half Jo Yapp, England established a 22-0 lead at the break and then piled on the points in a thrilling second half display to end the match as resounding 81-0 winners.

It was a remarkable performance, but England were brought back down to earth when they were then beaten 13-10 by France. Leading 10-8 after 80 minutes after an Appleby try,

England looked to have done enough to win, but the French side hit back with a dramatic match-winning touchdown deep into injury time. Defeat at such a late stage of the game was truly hard to swallow.

Richards' side proved they had bouncebackability, though, recovering to post 32 unanswered points in their next game against Ireland thanks to first half tries from Paula George, Kim Shaylor and Maggie Alphonsi, all of which provided a solid foundation for a solid win.

Next it was Spain's turn to suffer at England's hands as hat tricks for Captain Jo Yapp and Kim Shaylor, both of Worcester, led to a thumping 76-0 win at Imber Court.

In their final Six Nations fixture England battled to a 22-10 win over a committed Scotland side at Twickenham. The match marked Paula George's last game in an England jersey; she announced her retirement after the victory.

The season saw seven new caps, many coming through the system, in preparation for next year's

*Left:
Michaela
Staniford
makes her
presence felt
against Spain*

World Cup. It also produced a notable achievement for England full back Kim Shaylor, who ended the Six Nations tournament as top try scorer with nine touchdowns, grabbing second spot in the leading points scoring table.

England's women finished the season in May with a match against a touring South Africa side. In the first ever clash between the two countries England simply demolished their visitors 101-0, ending the campaign on yet another positive note.

Next season England will tour New Zealand in October to face Samoa and the All Blacks twice, while looking to regain the Six Nations crown so cruelly snatched away this year by France before their World Cup campaign in 2006.

*Left:
England's
forwards had
a superb
season*

WORDS: JIM BYERS. PICS: STEVE MITCHELL

ENGLAND COUNTIES

England Counties gave departing manager Rob Udwin the perfect send-off when they demolished France Amateurs 38-0 at Newbury in February 2005. Udwin handed over to Jim Robinson before this summer's trip to Argentina and Uruguay.

"The senior England side is now picked from the Premiership, which probably represents one per cent of the game in England; we represent the other 99 per cent," said Nelson. "It's still an evolving side, but it's a good standard of rugby. It sets the players the challenge of playing outside their club environment... and pulling on an England shirt, at whatever level you play, is a very proud moment."

The extent of that pride was evident against France Amateurs, a side the Counties had twice performed poorly against. This time round they swarmed all over an overworked defence that simply ran out of numbers to prevent full back Mal Roberts (twice), wings James Moore and James Aston, skipper Craig Hammond and replacement Warren Spragg from scoring the tries.

The seeds of that attacking approach were sown half a world away on the Pacific coast of Canada last year. The Counties ran in six tries in their 43-0 win against Vancouver Island Crimson Tide, then flew over the Rockies to score another half-dozen in beating the Canada Super League All Stars 38-17. The pick of the scores against the All Stars was an individual chip and chase effort from Moore, one of a handful of Counties players to appear in the Zurich Premiership in the last year.

He made his debut for Sale last season and Dean Schofield (Sale), Lee Fortey (Worcester) and Terry Sigley (Gloucester) have all progressed into the top flight since touring with the Counties.

In June Westage and Ryan continued to lead the counties to success, winning two out of three games on their South America tour. After a 10-36 defeat against an Argentine Provinces XV the England amateurs secured a 38-0 victory over Rosario. Another impressive performance clinched their most significant win to date against the Uruguay national team in Montevideo by 29-9, three of their five tries coming from unstoppable rolling mauls.

Pic: Sarah Williams

POWERGEN CHALLENGE SHIELD
INTERMEDIATE CUP & JUNIOR VASE

Leigh Hinton landed arguably the most important penalty of his career as Bedford banished 30 years of Twickenham blues to lift the Powergen Challenge Shield on April 16. Hinton recovered from three misses to kick the match winner in the 75th minute for a 14-13 victory over Plymouth Albion which gave Bedford their first senior cup triumph since they beat Rosslyn Park back in 1975.

The 26-year-old – whose merry-go-round career has included stints at Moseley, Orrell and now Bedford – kicked

ENGLAND STUDENTS & UNIVERSITIES

This season's England Students had a strong West Country flavour, with Bristol Shoguns coach Richard Hill on the sidelines and a large contingent of Gloucester's young stars in the team. At the end of the campaign Hill had claimed the National One title with the Shoguns and will doubtless run into some of his former pupils in the Guinness Premiership.

One of them will be Brad Davies, the Gloucester fly half who sent Kingsholm into orbit when his drop goal beat Bath in February.

A week earlier the Gloucester student was pulling the strings in England's 10-6 win over the French at Blackheath, a landmark result given the investment in this level of the game on the other side of the Channel.

The forwards battered France into giving away a penalty try, with Oxford's James Whittingham adding the conversion and a penalty.

It was a different story in the return game, where a beefed-up French side ground out a 23-6 win. But England rounded off the season in free-flowing style with a 27-27 draw against Italy at Oxford.

England made too many mistakes, but still excelled in attack with Mark Foster's injury time second try – converted by the reliable Whittingham – saving them from defeat.

The England Universities side – effectively the second tier students side – launched their season with a thrilling 17-11 win over their Australian counterparts, sealed by a last minute score from Oxford wing Jonan Boto. Their one defeat was a 38-10 setback against Wales at Pontypridd, but they recovered to beat Scotland 17-0, with two tries from Imperial Medics full back Huw Williams.

Their final outing was a 50-10 romp against the Combined Services Under 21s with fly half Stuart Alred – son of England kicking guru Dave Alred – slotting a penalty and five out of six conversion attempts. Dad would have been proud.

Left:
Adam Harris (Oxford) soars above the Italian lineout in the Students' 27-27 draw at Iffley Road

Far left:
Brad Davies (Gloucester) gets the ball away in the 10-6 win over France at Blackheath

Left:
Morley powered their way to Intermediate Cup victory over Westoe

all 15 points in the semi-final win over another former club, Pertemps Bees.

Morley claimed the Powergen Intermediate Cup in a 21-11 win over Westoe. Though Morley were ahead for most of the game, they had to withstand massive second half pressure before they could get their hands on the trophy. A second half drop goal from fly half Colin Stephens gave them the strength they needed to hold out.

Sheffield Tigers came from behind to beat Solihull 30-13 to win the Powergen Junior Vase for the second time after their first success in 2000.

WORDS: JIM BYERS

BRITISH UNIVERSITIES SPORTS ASSOCIATION

Women's Championship Final, Twickenham

Wednesday 27 April 2005
Loughborough 22
UWIC 20

Loughborough and UWIC, the two sides that have dominated the Women's championship over recent years, squared up in an epic encounter at Twickenham. A penalty from Alice Lovett with the very last kick of the game was just enough to retain the title for Loughborough, bringing to a close a thrilling finale that saw the lead dramatically change hands twice in injury time.

Men's Championship Final, Twickenham

Wednesday 27 April 2005
Loughborough 19
UWE Hartpury 16

This final never looked like reaching the dramatic climax of the women's match as the two sets of forwards locked horns in a titanic midfield struggle. UWE Hartpury fly half Rory Teague opened the scoring with a well-struck penalty,

although Loughborough were quick to respond with their opposite number Michael Glancy consistently finding space with his confident kicks to touch.

Loughborough then produced a dazzling 20 minutes of forward play, which ultimately proved to be the difference between the two sides. Two tries from prop Matthew Webber and a third from Benjamin Griffiths, along with two successful conversions from Glancy, pushed Loughborough into a good lead, ultimately going into the break 19-11 ahead.

The second half was dominated by forward play, with the game played almost entirely in the middle of the pitch. Hartpury had, however, learnt their lesson from the first half and tackled manfully to stop the Loughborough forwards from coming within striking distance of their line. Hartpury then crossed for a push over try of their own. Leo Halavatu forced his

way over from close range to get his side to within just three points of Loughborough. With almost 25 minutes remaining it looked like the gathered rain-sodden, bedraggled masses were in for another nail-biting climax. Nail-biting it was, but not in the same way as the preceding women's game, with the lone Hartpury try proving to be the only score of the second half. Despite some heavy late pressure and a couple of despairing drop goal attempts from Hartpury, Loughborough just managed to hold onto their lead to record a famous victory here and seal a momentous day for the University.

Right: Loughborough – BUSA men's champions

WORDS: ADAM WILD

ARMY V NAVY BABCOCK TROPHY

The Army won a fourth consecutive encounter at Twickenham when they secured the Babcock Trophy and overcame the Royal Navy by 41 points to 15 on Saturday 7 May. Only the Army, in 85 years of Inter Services rugby, have previously achieved four victories in a row.

The stirring rendition of the National Anthem by the hundred strong band of the Duke of York's School whetted the appetite for the 45,000 partisans present and emphasised the traditional intensity of this occasion.

The sun shone, the East Stand was warm, the pitch was red hot. At the first scrum the Reds submerged the Navy front row. Chris Budgen (Northampton Saints) and Steve Trethewey (Otley) gave their opposite numbers a torrid time and it took a huge effort from the Navy forwards to keep their ship afloat.

The Army were quick to launch further attacks and left wing Bruno Green (Newbury) and No 8 Isoa DamuDamu (Harlequins) were unlucky to be hauled down close to the line. Most importantly, the slick

interplay between the Army's forwards and backs set the strategic pattern for the match, with the Reds playing highly ambitious rugby.

The Navy controlled their lineouts well and fought hard for parity in the loose. In the early exchanges their forwards were effective at the maul and there were times when only stout defence kept the Army line intact. But even in their darker moments the Army team showed the sustained desire to counter-attack. England Counties locks Lee Soper (Launceston) and Andy Smith (Newbury) became increasingly

DAILY MAIL SCHOOLS DAY

A memorable Daily Mail Schools Day at Twickenham on Monday 22 March was the icing on the cake for this season's competitions, with glorious weather and exciting rugby combining to produce an excellent rugby occasion.

Pride of place went to Exeter College, who came from behind to claim a famous 25-23 win over St Peter's, York, with a try in injury-time to win the Daily Mail Under 18 Cup. This was the first time a Further Education establishment had won this major schools event.

Tenacity and self-belief was the key to Exeter's success after they trailed 20-5, with two tries by full back Ben Hough and one by scrum half James Pang, together with a conversion and a penalty from wingman Charlie Parry, putting St Peter's clear.

Centre Matt Hilton and flanker Jim Kelly made it 20-10 at the interval and a try from Morshead, followed by an exchange of penalties by fly half Glen Channing and Parry, set up a breathless finale with fullback Ben Scott grabbing the winning try.

St Benedict's, Ealing, ended another unblemished season in perfect fashion when they carried off the Daily Mail Under 15 Cup with a 12-7 win over their West London rivals St Paul's, Barnes. St Benedict's went ahead with a seventh-minute try from wingman Ivor Colson that fly half James Booth converted, but St Paul's No 8 and captain Chris Berry burst through for a try that fly half

Nicholas Simson goaled to level the scores.

St Benedict's struck the crucial blow, however, when, midway through the half, centre Adam Cole found just enough space to slip through for the winning try.

Pace and power were the crucial ingredients as Maidstone Grammar beat Oakham School 33-7 in the Daily Mail Under 15 Vase.

Crossley Heath, Halifax, were indebted to their watertight defence for helping them to lift the Daily Mail Under 18 Vase with a 10-3 win over St Joseph's, Stoke.

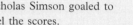

Left:
Exeter College celebrate their Daily Mail Under 18 Cup win

Below:
The Army lost this lineout, but won the match convincingly

---

dominant and, unable to regroup quickly, the Navy juggernaut ground to a virtual standstill.

For the last quarter the Navy were hard-pressed to achieve a degree of parity. Recent Fijian Sevens World Cup winner Apo Satala, an early focus for brave Navy defence, had a relatively quiet game, but compatriot DamuDamu at No 8 produced 80 minutes of fireworks.

Damu and back row replacements Ledua Jope and Taniela Delaitamana raced into the heart of a Navy defence, but there was little depth and no third phase cover. Once through the first line of defence Damu, Jope and Delaitamana, who scored two tries, were clean through.

As the Navy defence leaked, Soper and Smith found an extra yard of pace. Soper ran hard and leapt like a salmon to maintain the advantage. Smith, already recognised by the Barbarians, carried the ball with such determination that three blue shirts failed to stop him thundering under the posts for another score. Victory was secured.

Props Budgen and Trethewey and hooker George Kemble spent the first half of the season in Iraq. Their powerful performance reflected six months of gruelling dedication that started on the streets of Al-Amarah and ended at the Home of England Rugby.

Earlier in the season the Army beat the RAF 57-12 at Aldershot. In their first Inter Service win for eight years, a truly gallant RAF team led by the Barbarian Peter Taylor, beat the Navy 24-16 at Newbury.

ENGLAND RUGBY

Managing Editor **Howard Johnson**
Design **Steve Maddox, Joanna Legge**
Studio Manager **Malcolm Anderson**
Publisher **Paula Skinner**
Advertising Manager **Dan Grainger**
Advertising Sales Executive **Richard McIntyre**
Advertising Production **Tracey Killick**
Advertising Repro **Stephen Spicer**
Publishing Director **Jonathan Fellows**
Advertising Director **Charlie Wise**
Director **Andrew Stevens**

With special thanks to **Patricia Mowbray,
Richard Prescott, Dee McIntosh,
Jane Barron, James Bennett, Adrian Wolfe,
Jeremy Garman, Greg Newman
and Mostyn Thomas**

Printed by **Wyndeham Heron Ltd.**

Published by

TRMG Ltd
Winchester Court, 1 Forum Place, Hatfield, Herts AL10 0RN
Tel: 01707 273 999
Fax: 01707 276 555
www.trmg.co.uk
© 2005 TRMG Ltd